WEATHERED
encouragement through all seasons

~ 31 days of winter ~

Janelle Nobles

Copyright © 2014 by Janelle Nobles

All Scripture quotations, unless otherwise indicated, are taken from The Holy Bible, English Standard Version® (ESV®), copyright © 2001 by Crossway, a publishing ministry of Good News Publishers. Used by permission. All rights reserved.

Scripture quotations marked (AMP) are taken from the Amplified® Bible, Copyright © 1954, 1958, 1962, 1964, 1965, 1987 by The Lockman Foundation. Used by permission." (www.Lockman.org)

Scripture quotations marked (MSG) are taken from The Message. Copyright © 1993, 1994, 1995, 1996, 2000, 2001, 2002. Used by permission of NavPress Publishing Group.

Scripture quotations marked (NIV) are taken from THE HOLY BIBLE, NEW INTERNATIONAL VERSION®, NIV® Copyright © 1973, 1978, 1984, 2011 by Biblica, Inc.® Used by permission. All rights reserved worldwide.

Scripture quotations marked (NKJV) are taken from the New King James Version®. Copyright © 1982 by Thomas Nelson, Inc. Used by permission. All rights reserved.

Scripture quotations marked (NLT) are taken from the Holy Bible, New Living Translation, copyright © 1996, 2004, 2007 by Tyndale House Foundation. Used by permission of Tyndale House Publishers, Inc., Carol Stream, Illinois 60188. All rights reserved.

Scripture quotations marked (TLB) are taken from The Living Bible copyright © 1971. Used by permission of Tyndale House Publishers, Inc., Carol Stream, Illinois 60188. All rights reserved.

in His image productions
3276 Buford Drive
Suite 104-303
Buford, Georgia 30519
www.inhisimage.com

All rights reserved. No part of this publication may be reproduced, stored in a retrieval system, or transmitted in any form or by any means except for brief quotations in printed reviews, without the prior permission of the publisher.

ISBN-13: 978-1494866631
ISBN-10: 1494866633

First Edition: January 2014

~ winter ~
to my mom, Dena
thank you for making each season
of my life memorable

table of contents.

1. good night 3
2. storms 7
3. laundry 12
4. giants 15
5. dormant 19
6. wist list 23
7. reflection 27
8. windows 30
9. christmas 34
10. a girl 38
11. quilt 41
12. the valley 45
13. His glory 50
14. endurance 55
15. postcard 58
16. light in dark 62
17. cold season 66
18. budget 69
19. light & momentary 73
20. excuses 77
21. all of You 81
22. darkness singing 85
23. baby steps 90
24. comfort zone 95
25. sacrifice 99
26. scars 104
27. His image 110
28. signs 114
29. obedience 118
30. night season 122
31. come away 127
    verse index 135

INTRODUCTION

This set of devotionals has been a labor of love for you – my friend, my fellow mom, wife, and woman. I believe my journey has been similar to yours. We trek through singlehood, parenthood, and womanhood and venture in and out of seasons. Some of them we travel alone, some together.

I believe with all my heart that each season has its place and purpose. But the journey can be hard. And tiring. And lonely. It also can be amazing and full of wonder and revelation. Each is worth it.

The seasons I have experienced may not be the same as yours. My spring and autumn were flourishing and fruitful – speaking spiritually, some of the best times I can remember. Winter was a time of reflection and rest. The cold periods could be isolating but also a time of hope, knowing spring was about to burst onto the scene. Summer, for me, was definitely the longest and driest period I have ever faced. In fact, I have just emerged from a six-year stint in the summer wilderness. At times, I thought it would never end.

It did.

All seasons do.

This is my encouragement to you. There are no accidents. You are not in this season by chance. You will wander through some seasons with favor and awe, and others you will pray for relief and resolution. In your celebration, God is your cheerleader. In your defeat, He is your victory. In your loneliness, He is your love. In your gladness **and** grief, He is grace.

Grace for *all* seasons.

Winter is between autumn and spring and typically is the coldest season of the year in most climates. It is caused by the axis of the Earth in a specific hemisphere being oriented away from the Sun. In many regions, winter is equated with snow and freezing temperatures. At the winter solstice, the days are shortest and the nights are longest, with days lengthening as the season continues. For some, winter may evoke images of darkness and sadness or a warm coziness by the fireplace.

good night.

¹ Keep me safe, O God,
    for I have come to you for refuge.
² I said to the Lord, "You are my Master!
    Every good thing I have comes from you."
³ The godly people in the land
    are my true heroes!
    I take pleasure in them!
⁴ Troubles multiply for those who chase after other gods.
    I will not take part in their sacrifices of blood
    or even speak the names of their gods.
⁵ Lord, you alone are my inheritance, my cup of blessing.
    You guard all that is mine.
⁶ The land you have given me is a pleasant land.
    What a wonderful inheritance!
⁷ I will bless the Lord who guides me;
    even at night my heart instructs me.
⁸ I know the Lord is always with me.
    I will not be shaken, for he is right beside me.
⁹ No wonder my heart is glad, and I rejoice.
    My body rests in safety.
¹⁰ For you will not leave my soul among the dead
    or allow your holy one to rot in the grave.

[11] **You will show me the way of life,**
   granting me the joy of your presence
   and the pleasures of living with you forever.
-Psalm 16 (NLT)

Winter always brings longer hours of darkness. The winter solstice, which is the shortest day of the year and usually falls around December 21st (in the United States), has on average nine hours of daylight. That means in a 24-hour period there are 15 hours of darkness. That's a lot of darkness! And for some people that may cause a lot of sadness, apathy, or a mixture of both.

If you are blessed enough to live in Alaska, you will definitely have a more realistic understanding of an extended nighttime. There are some areas in northern Alaska where the sun sets in late August, and people do not see another sunrise until the following April. Yikes! That is a long winter!

This Psalm is perfect for those dark or night seasons. In fact, verse seven speaks directly to that very issue. We need something (or Someone) to guide us because it's dark and difficult to see. The Lord leads us as a shepherd would lead his flock at night.

Sheep have excellent peripheral vision, yet they have poor depth perception. As a result, they cannot see immediately in front of them. They require a shepherd, especially at night.

So do we.

Have you ever had to get up for something in the middle of the night? What about being aroused in a hotel room in the dead of night and forgetting where you are? How about waking up for no reason at two, three, four o'clock in the morning and replaying all the ways your life is screwed up (the enemy capitalizes on that one). I hate those feelings. Yet they seem to come and settle in during the darkest hours.

The Psalmist (King David, by the way) reminds us that the Lord is **always** with us. Verse eight evokes an image similar to an aide for a blind person or a shepherd for the sheep — He stays right beside us.

Imagine God being exactly like a guide, grasping our hand and wrapping it around His arm and not only leading us, but also being right beside us; all around us, all the time.

Because of His closeness to us, His holding on tightly and leading the way, we can rejoice and rest. The darkness is not quite so scary. The shadows are not quite so big. The blackness is not quite so bleak. We have hope.

Have you ever gone to the bathroom in the middle of the night and because you know the exact path you maneuver it on "auto-pilot?" (I literally can do it with my eyes closed.) What about the quietness of God waking you to pray for someone in the early hours before the sunrise? Have you ever sat under a pitch-black sky in absolute silence and marveled at what seems like a million stars? Those things happen in the dark seasons, as well.

So whatever things go bump in the night and whoever is trying to use darkness to terrify you, remember the One who holds your heart, night and day. His hands are big enough and strong enough and safe enough for all times.

Thank Him and have a good night.

WAIT: Imagine God wrapping your hand around His arm. He's got you.

CULTIVATE: Write this entire Psalm on a card and keep it on the fridge, in your car, or in a place you can read it daily as you journey through this season.

storms.

[1] I love you, Lord;
    you are my strength.
[2] The Lord is my rock, my fortress, and my savior;
    my God is my rock, in whom I find protection.
  He is my shield, the power that saves me,
    and my place of safety.
[3] I called on the Lord, who is worthy of praise,
    and he saved me from my enemies.

[4] The ropes of death entangled me;
    floods of destruction swept over me.
[5] The grave wrapped its ropes around me;
    death laid a trap in my path.
[6] But in my distress I cried out to the Lord;
    yes, I prayed to my God for help.
  He heard me from his sanctuary;
    my cry to him reached his ears.

[7] Then the earth quaked and trembled.
    The foundations of the mountains shook;
    they quaked because of his anger.

⁸ Smoke poured from his nostrils;
　　fierce flames leaped from his mouth.
　　Glowing coals blazed forth from him.
⁹ He opened the heavens and came down;
　　dark storm clouds were beneath his feet.
¹⁰ Mounted on a mighty angelic being, he flew,
　　soaring on the wings of the wind.
¹¹ He shrouded himself in darkness,
　　veiling his approach with dark rain clouds.
¹² Thick clouds shielded the brightness around him
　　and rained down hail and burning coals.
¹³ The Lord thundered from heaven;
　　the voice of the Most High resounded
　　amid the hail and burning coals.
¹⁴ He shot his arrows and scattered his enemies;
　　his lightning flashed, and they were greatly confused.
¹⁵ Then at your command, O Lord,
　　at the blast of your breath,
　the bottom of the sea could be seen,
　　and the foundations of the earth were laid bare.
¹⁶ He reached down from heaven and rescued me;
　　he drew me out of deep waters.
¹⁷ He rescued me from my powerful enemies,
　　from those who hated me and were too strong for me.
¹⁸ They attacked me at a moment when I was in distress,
　　but the Lord supported me.

[19] He led me to a place of safety;
   he rescued me because he delights in me.
-Psalm 18:1-19 (NLT)

The forecast for the rest of this week is cloudy with a 70% chance of rain. There is not one sun icon on the weatherman's five-day outlook. I hate seeing the cloud icon. No sun in sight.

My moods are, at times, influenced by the weather. Ok, most of the time. I subconsciously decide what kind of day it's going to be by the image I see outside my bedroom window in the morning. A bright, sunny morning can make me move a little bit faster and keep me smiling a little longer. If I awake to the sound of raindrops hitting the roof and darkness looming at my window, I automatically resign myself to a depressed state of mind. How stupid is that?

To look at life through my eyes only hinders the majesty of what God can do in and through me any given day. We have come to associate sunshine with happiness, and rain with depression. Keep in mind, however, God is the Creator of both. There are reasons and seasons for both.

This Psalm directs us in the first stanza, to focus our attention on God. He is our fortress, our savior, our shield, and our protection. As I am waking up, my mind should be directed toward the day God has given me, regardless of the weather. I need to call on Him; especially considering the next set of verses.

The following stanza is filled with images of depression. (I have, at times, felt like death was entangling me. Feelings of destruction have often swept over me for no apparent reason.) And again, the Psalmist cries out to the Lord. The attention has to be taken off the exterior situations in my life and placed upon God as my help.

What is fascinating to me is the fashion of His entrance that happens in verse 11. He shrouds Himself in darkness. He is in the darkness! His approach is veiled by dark storm clouds. Do you see that? He is in the storm!

His voice is amidst the thunder and hail. When we see only with our earthly eyes, we may miss Him. He engages us in a heavenly manner. We often see sadness, darkness, and depression, but He is bigger than all of the clouds. He reaches down to rescue us from the sadness, darkness, and depression.

He draws us out, rescues us, and supports us because He delights in us. He does not come because we call – but we should call. He does not come because we cry out – though we should cry out. He simply comes because He delights in us… in me… and in you.

No matter what the forecast, know this – the Lord is in it all! He delights in you whether there is a thunderstorm warning or sunny skies ahead.

WAIT: Whatever weather is happening outside, go out and sit under God's greatness.

CULTIVATE: Get some fresh sunflowers and put them in a prominent place as a reminder of God's favor on all of your days.

laundry.

"Look! I'm sending my messenger on ahead to clear the way for me. Suddenly, out of the blue, the Leader you've been looking for will enter his Temple – yes, the Messenger of the Covenant, the one you've been waiting for. Look! He's on his way!" A Message from the mouth of God-of-the-Angel-Armies.

But who will be able to stand up to that coming? Who can survive his appearance?

He'll be like white-hot fire from the smelter's furnace. He'll be like the strongest lye soap at the laundry. He'll take his place as a refiner of silver, as a cleanser of dirty clothes. He'll scrub the Levite priests clean, refine them like gold and silver, until they're fit for God, fit to present offerings of righteousness. Then, and only then, will Judah and Jerusalem be fit and pleasing to God, as they used to be in the years long ago.
-Malachi 3:1-4 (MSG)

Right now I am sitting on the floor in my laundry room watching the clothes spin in the dryer. I hate washing clothes. If there is one household chore I dread, it is washing clothes. Probably because the dirty clothes hampers in my house are never empty.

My husband bought me a nice, new washer and dryer set – the front loader kind with the awesome drawer on the bottom. They are black and stylish. They hold more clothes, so I have fewer loads to wash… but I still hate laundry!

In fact, for me it's depressing. As I sit here and look at mounds of clothes, socks and underwear I wonder how we can get so many things dirty. Mysterious stains show up – always on the white shirts. A piece of paper sneaks in and creates a confetti party amongst the towels. And a hidden bite-sized candy bar completely makes its hiding place known… melted on the inside of a pant pocket. Yuck! I want to cry…

I can't imagine what God's laundry room looks like. Must be depressing – in fact, I'm getting more down in the dumps just thinking about it. I know my clothes are covered with stains – some I'm aware of and others… well, I'm not even sure how they got there. I DO know I left that wadded up tissue in the hamper, from when I had a pity party (like now) and dried my eyes and nose.

You know what I just realized? God hates laundry, too!

He despises looking at my never-ending pile of dirty clothes. Just when He gets my stuff clean, I'm getting something else dirty. But, I'm so glad He doesn't give up on the job. I guess I won't either. The dryer is buzzing… gotta go.

WAIT: God never tires of making us clean. Read Psalm 51.

CULTIVATE: Do laundry or wash dishes today, and rest in the fact of Jesus washing our hearts clean – daily.

giants.

[36] Your servant has killed both lion and bear; and this uncircumcised Philistine will be like one of them, seeing he has defied the armies of the living God." [37] Moreover David said, "The Lord, who delivered me from the paw of the lion and from the paw of the bear, He will deliver me from the hand of this Philistine."

And Saul said to David, "Go, and the Lord be with you!"

[38] So Saul clothed David with his armor, and he put a bronze helmet on his head; he also clothed him with a coat of mail. [39] David fastened his sword to his armor and tried to walk, for he had not tested them. And David said to Saul, "I cannot walk with these, for I have not tested them." So David took them off.

[40] Then he took his staff in his hand; and he chose for himself five smooth stones from the brook, and put them in a shepherd's bag, in a pouch which he had, and his sling was in his hand. And he drew near to the Philistine. [41] So the Philistine came, and began drawing near to David, and the man who bore the shield went before him. [42] And when

the Philistine looked about and saw David, he disdained him; for he was only a youth, ruddy and good-looking. ⁴³So the Philistine said to David, "Am I a dog, that you come to me with sticks?" And the Philistine cursed David by his gods. ⁴⁴ And the Philistine said to David, "Come to me, and I will give your flesh to the birds of the air and the beasts of the field!"

⁴⁵ Then David said to the Philistine, "You come to me with a sword, with a spear, and with a javelin. But I come to you in the name of the Lord of hosts, the God of the armies of Israel, whom you have defied. ⁴⁶ This day the Lord will deliver you into my hand, and I will strike you and take your head from you. And this day I will give the carcasses of the camp of the Philistines to the birds of the air and the wild beasts of the earth, that all the earth may know that there is a God in Israel. ⁴⁷ Then all this assembly shall know that the Lord does not save with sword and spear; for the battle is the Lord's, and He will give you into our hands."

⁴⁸ So it was, when the Philistine arose and came and drew near to meet David, that David hurried and ran toward the army to meet the Philistine. ⁴⁹ Then David put his hand in his bag and took out a stone; and he slung it and struck the Philistine in his forehead, so that the stone sank into his forehead, and he fell on his face to the earth.

[50] So David prevailed over the Philistine with a sling and a stone, and struck the Philistine and killed him. But there was no sword in the hand of David. [51] Therefore David ran and stood over the Philistine, took his sword and drew it out of its sheath and killed him, and cut off his head with it.

And when the Philistines saw that their champion was dead, they fled.
-1 Samuel 17:36-51 (NKJV)

Giants are walking among us constantly. Some giants are financial trouble caused by overwhelming debt. Others take the form of struggling marriages. Still other giants could be troubled teen issues, ailing and aging parents, or career crossroads. We live with giants, but we don't have to be overwhelmed by them.

When David faced Goliath, he did not focus on how big or how strong the giant was. David acknowledged he had faced very difficult situations before with the lion and the beast. He also recognized publically the One who had pulled him through – God. David took no credit for overcoming. And so, he put his faith in what he knew as he faced yet another "giant".

In 1 Samuel 17, we read about David using a stone and sling to slay Goliath; a small, insignificant weapon to take down a huge giant and threat. David wanted to make sure God got the credit for this slaying.

God wants the same in our lives.

If we are able to take care of the giants we face – whether physically, emotionally or practically – God may not be given the credit. And believe me, He wants the credit!

Don't try to use the "best" weapons available to beat the giants yourself. Instead, pick up a stone and a sling and trust in "the Lord of hosts" to slay your giants. And listen closely for the thud as it falls.

WAIT: What is a "giant" that you are facing today?

CULTIVATE: Write down a "giant" in your past that God has slain and remind yourself today that He can and will do it again.

dormant.

⁶ As you have therefore received Christ, [even] Jesus the Lord, [so] walk (regulate your lives and conduct yourselves) in union with and conformity to Him.

⁷ Have the roots [of your being] firmly and deeply planted [in Him, fixed and founded in Him], being continually built up in Him, becoming increasingly more confirmed and established in the faith, just as you were taught, and abounding and overflowing in it with thanksgiving.

⁸ See to it that no one carries you off as spoil or makes you yourselves captive by his so-called philosophy and intellectualism and vain deceit (idle fancies and plain nonsense), following human tradition (men's ideas of the material rather than the spiritual world), just crude notions following the rudimentary and elemental teachings of the universe and disregarding [the teachings of] Christ (the Messiah).

⁹ For in Him the whole fullness of Deity (the Godhead) continues to dwell in bodily form [giving complete expression of the divine nature].

¹⁰ And you are in Him, made full and having come to fullness of life [in Christ you too are filled with the Godhead--Father, Son and Holy Spirit--and reach full spiritual stature]. And He is the Head of all rule and authority [of every angelic principality and power].
-Colossians 2:6-10 (AMP)

I love the colors of fall; spectacular orange, red, and gold leaves exploding on acres of treetops. It is truly one of my favorite sights.

As I sit here in the dead of winter peering out my window I am not inspired. The trees are bare and lifeless. Even the evergreens are muted. There is little vibrancy and fewer splendors. However, God prompted me to look closer.

My perspective of the winter tree is from afar, but the feeling of coldness is close to my soul. Most trees are empty – void of leaves, flowers, or fruit. In our wintry seasons we can have a tendency to feel empty – like a bare house with no heat. Tree trunks appear dull in color. The deep, brown bark has faded to a somber gray. Likewise, we give off a discouraged countenance in the midst of our own emotional winter. We envision branches with no fruit. We experience turbulent winds and storms. The ground beneath us seems icy and dead.

Our earthly senses feel, experience, and see. In contrast, what is **not** visible are the roots that grow deep. The fruit bearing seeds are not tangible… yet. During this time God deepens our faith in Him. Our perseverance through the bitter cold strengthens our roots in Christ. Look closely at a dormant tree, and you may catch a glimpse of spring buds – the beginning of something new. Jesus gives the illustration of the fig tree in Matthew 24:32:

> "Take a lesson from the fig tree. From the moment you notice its buds form, the merest hint of green, you know summer's just around the corner. So it is with you: When you see all these things, you'll know he's at the door. Don't take this lightly." (MSG)

Winter is necessary in order to welcome spring. Throughout the bitter times in our lives God is not only carrying us, He is cultivating us for something greater. So, understand as the winds blow and the winter sets in, you must dig your roots down deep – deep within the ground of God's goodness.

WAIT: Read verse seven again, and know He is strengthening and establishing your roots.

CULTIVATE: Actually plant a bulb – a tulip, a daffodil, or an iris. Realize that you may not see any bloom for a season or two, but work is being done underground – and so in your heart.

wish list.

[25] "Therefore I tell you, do not be anxious about your life, what you will eat or what you will drink, nor about your body, what you will put on. Is not life more than food, and the body more than clothing? [26] Look at the birds of the air: they neither sow nor reap nor gather into barns, and yet your heavenly Father feeds them. Are you not of more value than they? [27] And which of you by being anxious can add a single hour to his span of life?

[28] And why are you anxious about clothing? Consider the lilies of the field, how they grow: they neither toil nor spin, [29] yet I tell you, even Solomon in all his glory was not arrayed like one of these. [30] But if God so clothes the grass of the field, which today is alive and tomorrow is thrown into the oven, will he not much more clothe you, O you of little faith?

[31] Therefore do not be anxious, saying, 'What shall we eat?' or 'What shall we drink?' or 'What shall we wear?' [32] For the Gentiles seek after all these things, and your heavenly Father knows that you need them all. [33] But seek first the kingdom of God and his righteousness, and all these things will be

added to you.
-Matthew 6:25-33 (NLT)

18-20 And now I have it all—and keep getting more! The gifts you sent with Epaphroditus were more than enough, like a sweet-smelling sacrifice roasting on the altar, filling the air with fragrance, pleasing God no end. You can be sure that God will take care of everything you need, his generosity exceeding even yours in the glory that pours from Jesus. Our God and Father abounds in glory that just pours out into eternity. Yes.
-Philippians 4:18-20 (MSG)

When my oldest son, Reece, was only one and half we traveled to my hometown of Chattanooga from Texas. We were excited to be able to enjoy the cold weather (not felt much in Austin) and the delight of a big family holiday. Reece was the only grandson and great-grandson on both sides of our families. Therefore, every aunt and uncle and grandparent was anxious to experience the excitement of a toddler and toys.

My dad's home was buzzing with happiness on Christmas Day. There were tempting scents emerging from the kitchen (which told us sausage balls and cookies were close at hand);

brightly colored packages were overflowing underneath the decorated tree; music and laughter filled the atmosphere. It was good to be back home with family and tradition.

Finally, the time came to open gifts. Of course, Reece was the center of attention because who really cares to watch an adult unwrap a set of dishes. Boring! A child's look of wonder and the thrill of ripping wrapping paper is much more entertaining.

Reece received a truck, talking books, and a tricycle just his size. He decided to open the remainder of his presents as he sat on the tricycle… who wouldn't? My dad handed him a box.

Oh, no! I knew the shape of the box, and I foresaw a terrible reaction. It was a shirt-sized box, which meant clothes. NO toddler wants clothes.

He proceeded to tear off the paper with anticipation. As he lifted the lid his brow furrowed and a look of disgust appeared on his angelic face. The entire family burst out in laughter. They weren't offended. Everyone was totally aware that no kid wants something he **needs**. He wanted the good stuff. The fun stuff.

So do we.

Our wish list for God usually consists of a promotion, a pleasurable vacation, or some peace and quiet. We seek things of comfort or contentment. However, we do not always get what we want.

Sometimes we get the shirt box. And that's ok.

Every Christmas, I give my children wonderful gifts that they carefully categorize on their wish list, but they always get stuff they need. Like a toothbrush. Or socks and underwear. Or clothes.

The Father also doesn't always give us the fun and fanciful things on our list. Our needs are His first priority – holiness, sanctification, and redemption. According to verse 30, He clothes us. Like the flowers of the field, we must trust His judgment. We must unwrap the gift He has chosen for us, even if it's not on our wish list.

Even if it's in a shirt box.

*WAIT: Trust God today for things you **need**, not just for things on your "wish list."*

*CULTIVATE: As you pray today, truly evaluate your requests to the Lord. Write down five things you **need** from the Lord – patience, better attitude, faith, forgiving heart, or endurance.*

reflection.

²⁵ My earthly life cleaves to the dust; revive and stimulate me according to Your word!

²⁶ I have declared my ways and opened my griefs to You, and You listened to me; teach me Your statutes.

²⁷ Make me understand the way of Your precepts; so shall I meditate on and talk of Your wondrous works.

²⁸ My life dissolves and weeps itself away for heaviness; raise me up and strengthen me according to [the promises of] Your word.

²⁹ Remove from me the way of falsehood and unfaithfulness [to You], and graciously impart Your law to me.

³⁰ I have chosen the way of truth and faithfulness; Your ordinances have I set before me.

³¹ I cleave to Your testimonies; O Lord, put me not to shame!

³² I will [not merely walk, but] run the way of Your commandments, when You give me a heart that is willing.

-Psalm 119:25-32 (AMP)

A season of dryness has been lingering in my life for an extended period of time. I have felt parched and thirsty; never really feeling fully satisfied. I have my quiet times, read books, listen to the occasional online message – all this while being very active in my church. But still feeling like a desert - with not even a mirage in sight.

Wintry, yet dry; that is my current environment.

(Just a side note… Polar or arctic deserts actually do exist. They are characterized by receiving less than 10 inches of precipitation and never rising above 50 degrees Fahrenheit. In fact, the Antarctica Desert is the largest desert in the world. A cold desert.)

One day during some prayer time I had a thought. I wasn't even really praying. I was finished with my prayers and just waiting. Kind of waiting on God, and kind of procrastinating to get the day started. The "thought" was more of a reflection. I felt like the Lord was saying, "You are not in the desert. You are by the water. Right now I don't want you to drink it, though – I want you to really look at it. Look deep into it. Reflect on it. Reflect."

The season I was in was a time of reflection. Not a time of thinking about myself necessarily, but a time of meditating on God's Word, God's grace, God's character. That was where I was. Standing by a clear, calm pool of water looking at my reflection, but seeing past the image. Actually engrossed in the water itself and all its attributes.

Well, my whole attitude changed from that moment on. It was amazing how my perception of my position chartered the course for each day. I had been living each day in the desert because it's where I **thought** I was. And maybe I was, and the Lord moved me. But I have a feeling I had been at this pool of water for a while. God was probably trying to get my attention. I kept looking around at my circumstances, instead of right beside me and past the image of myself. He changed my focus from near to become far; taking my focal point deeper to see His image rather than my own.

I don't quite feel so thirsty anymore.

WAIT: What things have you been focusing on for too long? God may want to change your vision and shift your focus.

CULTIVATE: Reflect on God's Word this week. Read all of Psalm 119.

windows.

16-17 "'Everyone who hurt you will be hurt;
 your enemies will end up as slaves.
Your plunderers will be plundered;
 your looters will become loot.
As for you, I'll come with healing,
 curing the incurable,
Because they all gave up on you
 and dismissed you as hopeless—
 that good-for-nothing Zion.'

18-21 "Again, God's Message:
 "'I'll turn things around for Jacob.
 I'll compassionately come in and rebuild homes.
The town will be rebuilt on its old foundations;
 the mansions will be splendid again.
Thanksgivings will pour out of the windows;
 laughter will spill through the doors.
Things will get better and better.
 Depression days are over.
They'll thrive, they'll flourish.
 The days of contempt will be over.
They'll look forward to having children again,

to being a community in which I take pride.
I'll punish anyone who hurts them,
   and their prince will come from their own ranks.
One of their own people shall be their leader.
   Their ruler will come from their own ranks.
I'll grant him free and easy access to me.
   Would anyone dare to do that on his own,
   to enter my presence uninvited?'
-Jeremiah 30:17-21 (MSG)

I have just opened my windows to let in the first cool breezes after a hot summer. Clouds are overhead, and storms are coming. The wind on the front side of this cold front is a welcome relief to the humidity and heat.

As the breeze gently blows the curtains and the trees quietly rustle outside, the Lord sweetly reminds me that "opening the windows" is exactly what I should do more often.

Windows are only mentioned 43 times in the Bible (King James Version). About 20% of the time, specific information is given regarding window dimensions when building the temple. The other references to windows are much more interesting.

Throughout scripture, windows represent hope (Noah's ark), escape (Rahab in Jeremiah 2:21), and blessing (Malachi 3:10). A window is actually something more. Think about a window in your home. Plain or decorative, it is a barrier from the elements, yet an "opening" revealing what is on the outside. This imagery is magical and spiritual.

We, as Americans, have arrived at a time of keeping our "windows" closed. With the advancement of indoor heating and cooling, we strive to remain comfortable by setting the thermostat and walking away. Simple. Easy. Deceiving.

We set the temperature within our spiritual lives, as well. We go to church, put in our 15 minutes of devotional time (maybe), and we listen to Christian radio. We set the thermostat of our lives and walk away, assuming things will remain comfortable. Well, windows are meant to be opened, and life is meant to be stirred up!

Daniel 6:10 caught my attention this morning (once I opened my own windows). King Darius had been tricked into signing a law, which prohibited anyone in the kingdom from praying to anyone other than him. Once the law was signed, Daniel went home and prayed to the Living God of Israel. Here is the interesting part; the Bible specifically says, "with his windows open." Daniel probably could have felt safer if the windows were closed, but I believe he knew something...

Opening windows invites the presence and blessing of God.

Today, whether it's sunny or raining, cold or hot, take an opportunity to "open a window". Do something "in the natural" in order to encourage something supernatural. "Thanksgivings will pour out of the windows; laughter will spill through the doors."

WAIT: Think about a spiritual window you need to open in your life.

CULTIVATE: Go open a window! Do it – even if it's the middle of winter. Sit and read God's Word as His spirit refreshes yours.

christmas.

[25] Now there was a man in Jerusalem called Simeon, who was righteous and devout. He was waiting for the consolation of Israel, and the Holy Spirit was upon him. [26] It had been revealed to him by the Holy Spirit that he would not die before he had seen the Lord's Christ. [27] Moved by the Spirit, he went into the temple courts. When the parents brought in the child Jesus to do for him what the custom of the Law required, [28] Simeon took him in his arms and praised God, saying:

[29] "Sovereign Lord, as you have promised,
   you now dismiss your servant in peace.
[30] For my eyes have seen your salvation,
   31which you have prepared in the sight of all people,
[32] a light for revelation to the Gentiles
   and for glory to your people Israel."

[33] The child's father and mother marveled at what was said about him. [34] Then Simeon blessed them and said to Mary, his mother: "This child is destined to cause the falling and rising of many in Israel, and to be a sign that will be spoken against, [35] so that the thoughts of many hearts will be revealed. And a sword will pierce your own soul too."

[36] There was also a prophetess, Anna, the daughter of Phanuel, of the tribe of Asher. She was very old; she had lived with her husband seven years after her marriage, [37] and then was a widow until she was eighty-four. She never left the temple but worshiped night and day, fasting and praying. [38] Coming up to them at that very moment, she gave thanks to God and spoke about the child to all who were looking forward to the redemption of Jerusalem.
-Luke 2:25-38 (NIV)

I have birthed four children, so I know something about the anticipation of labor and delivery. As my belly became larger my soul swelled with expectation. However, after my first son I realized giving birth was somewhat of an unknown expectancy.

I expected "something" – a baby, an addition to our family, a new life. But I also expected something more… an adventure, a sacred experience, a divine intervention. I knew there would be pain, but I was prepared. I knew it would be demanding; yet I was determined. I knew it would be exhausting, and I was so excited. The birth of a child is always full of anticipation – whether you adopt or physically birth the person whom God has chosen for your life.

And so it is with Jesus.

As the holiday season approaches, God has stirred something in my spirit. Something different this year. Amidst the mall decorations and the barrage of commercials for "stuff", the Lord gently reminded me of the excitement and expectation leading up to the birth of Christ. Even the Scriptures tell us certain Jews (Simeon and Anna) were waiting and watchful. People (and angels) were on the edge of their seats. They were excited. They were expectant. How cool is that?

I believe God wants us to have that kind of excitement every Christmas season (actually every day).

I enjoy all the tradition and all the magic during the holidays. I bake cookies, decorate every room, and listen to Christmas music non-stop. In the same way, I immersed myself in preparing for each child while I was pregnant. We decorated a nursery, amassed adorable clothes, and organized the house for each child's arrival. The preparation and enthusiasm went hand in hand.

So… at Christmas, we still situate our spirits in a state of preparation and enthusiasm. The Savior of the world is celebrated.

Just as we plan our own child's birthday, we should plan for the

King's arrival. Plan and prepare your heart to truly remember and celebrate Jesus' birthday. His arrival was the greatest gift heaven and earth has known. His humble entrance into our world was a call for angels to sing and rejoice. His miraculous advent was exactly what our souls were expecting.

Jesus coming to earth to serve and save and saturate our lives with grace. What a gift!

So… prepare, ponder, praise.

WAIT: Celebrate Christmas in your heart today no matter the time of year.

CULTIVATE: Write a to-do list for the advent in your heart. How can you prepare yourself for Jesus to show up bigger and brighter this week? Do some spiritual nesting!

a girl.

---

26 In the sixth month the angel Gabriel was sent from God to a city of Galilee named Nazareth, 27 to a virgin betrothed to a man whose name was Joseph, of the house of David. And the virgin's name was Mary. 28 And he came to her and said, "Greetings, O favored one, the Lord is with you!" 29 But she was greatly troubled at the saying, and tried to discern what sort of greeting this might be. 30 And the angel said to her, "Do not be afraid, Mary, for you have found favor with God. 31 And behold, you will conceive in your womb and bear a son, and you shall call his name Jesus. 32 He will be great and will be called the Son of the Most High. And the Lord God will give to him the throne of his father David, 33 and he will reign over the house of Jacob forever, and of his kingdom there will be no end."

34 And Mary said to the angel, "How will this be, since I am a virgin?"

35 And the angel answered her, "The Holy Spirit will come upon you, and the power of the Most High will overshadow you; therefore the child to be born will be called holy— the Son of God. 36 And behold, your relative Elizabeth in

her old age has also conceived a son, and this is the sixth month with her who was called barren. [37] For nothing will be impossible with God."
-Luke 1:26-37 (ESV)

[41] When Elizabeth heard Mary's greeting, the baby leaped in her womb, and Elizabeth was filled with the Holy Spirit. [42] In a loud voice she exclaimed: "Blessed are you among women, and blessed is the child you will bear!"
-Luke 1:41-42 (NIV)

[46] Mary responded,
  "Oh, how my soul praises the Lord.
[47] How my spirit rejoices in God my Savior!
[48] For he took notice of his lowly servant girl,
  and from now on all generations will call me blessed.
[49] For the Mighty One is holy,
  and he has done great things for me.
-Luke 1:46-49 (NLT)

a girl
an angel
a message
a blessing
a baby

to behold
to bring
to bless
to believe
to be

light
truth
peace
hope
savior

saving
loving
forgiving
holding
giving

a gift to you
from God
using… a girl

by Janelle Nobles

quilt.

Oh yes, you shaped me first inside, then out;
    you formed me in my mother's womb.
I thank you, High God—you're breathtaking!
    Body and soul, I am marvelously made!
    I worship in adoration—what a creation!
You know me inside and out,
    you know every bone in my body;
You know exactly how I was made, bit by bit,
    how I was sculpted from nothing into something.
Like an open book,
    you watched me grow from conception to birth;
    all the stages of my life were spread out before you,
The days of my life all prepared
    before I'd even lived one day.
-Psalm 139:13-16 (MSG)

[13] The Lord looks down from heaven;
    he sees all the children of man;
[14] from where he sits enthroned he looks out
    on all the inhabitants of the earth,
[15] he who fashions the hearts of them all
    and observes all their deeds.

[16] The king is not saved by his great army;
   a warrior is not delivered by his great strength.
[17] The war horse is a false hope for salvation,
   and by its great might it cannot rescue.
[18] Behold, the eye of the Lord is on those who fear him,
   on those who hope in his steadfast love,
[19] that he may deliver their soul from death
   and keep them alive in famine.
[20] Our soul waits for the Lord;
   he is our help and our shield.
[21] For our heart is glad in him,
   because we trust in his holy name.
[22] Let your steadfast love, O Lord, be upon us,
   even as we hope in you.
-Psalm 33:13-22 (ESV)

I am truly a patchwork quilt. We all are. I took a quilting class years ago before I had four children who demanded 26 hours of my 24-hour day. That quilting class was tough. I had to use the correct fabric, choose a harmony of colors, and purchase the correct tools. I had to learn how to cut blocks, hand sew pieces, and finish with binding. After twelve weeks of classes, and many elderly women helping me, I successfully finished my first child's baby quilt.

Since then I have received a wonderful quilt from my mother-in-law, and I've been given a "scrap" quilt that my mother found at a rummage sale. I truly love looking at them. I think they are a marvelous work of art.

My life is like a quilt that God has started and is continuing to work on. The fabric of my quilt is definitely full of scraps. I have a beautiful piece stained with my great-grandmother's blackberry cobbler. Several blocks are maroon and gold reminding me of my high school friends and folly. Many pieces are tear-stained from deaths, divorce, and disappointments. Countless segments have been added since my salvation. Pieces to remind me of God's grace, faithfulness, and love.

I look at my quilt and admire the handiwork. I'm certain it is an item that would be passed over at an auction. It definitely does not reflect royalty as some wedding quilts (however a great Bridegroom has contributed to the making). The pattern looks somewhat haphazard, but it has been thoughtfully designed. Edges are worn. Some colors have faded. Many stains remain. This quilt is not manufactured for mass production – it is a one-of-a-kind.

You are also being sewn by the master's hand. The joys and sorrows, the tears and sweat, the past and present – each of these is lending itself to a beautiful and unique pattern.

Look back on your past, especially the rough times and picture how they have enhanced this work of art. Think about the season you are in right now – how is it adding exceptional beauty to the masterpiece? Spend some time admiring the work and rest in knowing the Lord is still cutting, patching, and sewing.

It is a work in progress – full of splendor. And priceless!

WAIT: Reflect on all the pieces that make up your "quilt."

CULTIVATE: Consider buying or sewing a quilt (even a small one). Choose one carefully as you admire the various fabrics and textures.

the valley.

[1] The Lord is my shepherd;
   I have all that I need.
[2] He lets me rest in green meadows;
   he leads me beside peaceful streams.
[3] He renews my strength.
He guides me along right paths,
   bringing honor to his name.
[4] Even when I walk
   through the darkest valley,
I will not be afraid,
   for you are close beside me.
Your rod and your staff
   protect and comfort me.
[5] You prepare a feast for me
   in the presence of my enemies.
You honor me by anointing my head with oil.
   My cup overflows with blessings.
[6] Surely your goodness and unfailing love will pursue me
   all the days of my life,
and I will live in the house of the Lord forever.
-Psalm 23 (NLT)

¹⁷ "When the poor and needy search for water and there is none,
    and their tongues are parched from thirst,
then I, the Lord, will answer them.
    I, the God of Israel, will never abandon them.
¹⁸ I will open up rivers for them on the high plateaus.
    I will give them fountains of water in the valleys.
I will fill the desert with pools of water.
    Rivers fed by springs will flow across the parched ground.
¹⁹ I will plant trees in the barren desert—
    cedar, acacia, myrtle, olive, cypress, fir, and pine.
²⁰ I am doing this so all who see this miracle
    will understand what it means—
that it is the Lord who has done this,
    the Holy One of Israel who created it.
-Isaiah 41:17-20 (NLT)

I have responsibilities – wife, mom, work, church volunteer, and teacher. Those are just a few of the jobs that I juggle on a weekly basis. I've come to the realization that the people in my life **expect** me to function at "full," even when I feel like I'm on empty.

I've settled into a place I call "the valley." Peaks and promises can be seen from my low vantage point, but I am not a willing participant. Life is happening all around me, but I am only going through the motions (and sometimes at a snail's pace). Serving, working, and living to keep the charade up – a game I have come to play quite well.

Valley: *a low area of land between hills or mountains, typically with a river or stream flowing through it.*

I *know* I'm in a low season right now. I *know* this is exactly where God wants me (just unsure how long). And, I *know* Jesus is with me. These things I *know*. I do not like it, and I've made that clear to the Lord. My heart and mind are constantly discouraged, disappointed, and disengaged. But… It's where He has me. For now.

Here is what I have learned living in the valley:
- God is here – whether I *feel* His presence or not
- He provides for me – even when I cannot pray, read, or reach out
- Time in the valley is NOT based on my performance – God sets the times and seasons in my life
- His grace is sufficient – no matter what the circumstances
- My time in the valley produces beloved dependency on the Father

I love Jesus. My church is fantastic, and my family and

friends are awesome. I have shelter, food, clothing, books, heat, a phone, a bed, and so many more things thought to be necessities. I live in an amazing country where I am free to work, worship, and speak my mind. Yet, no one told me I'd spend so much time in the valley. In the midst of a "good" life, I plunged into a canyon of sorrow (for no apparent reason). While all appears wonderful on the outside, it is wretched on the inside.

In the valley.

This is the exact time to trust God; while in the valley. Know He's there, stand on His Word, and rest in His plan; while in the valley. Do not look too long or too often at people on the peaks. Do not focus on the factors of why, how, and when you arrived. Do not contemplate what is on the other side or if the grass is greener. It may be (or it may be AstroTurf). Just know, stand, and rest. In the valley.

When the Lord is ready for you to move on, He'll make a way out. Most valleys typically have a river running through them. Draw from it. He will and can renew you, refresh you, and restore you.

In the valley.

WAIT: Contemplate where you are during this time – the valley, the mountaintop, or somewhere in between?

CULTIVATE: Read Isaiah 41 and Psalm 23 again. God is intentional in setting the times and seasons in our own lives (Daniel 2:21). Know, stand, and rest in the valley.

His glory.

¹ But now, thus says the Lord, who created you, O Jacob,
And He who formed you, O Israel:
"Fear not, for I have redeemed you;
I have called you by your name;
You are Mine.
² When you pass through the waters, I will be with you;
And through the rivers, they shall not overflow you.
When you walk through the fire, you shall not be burned,
Nor shall the flame scorch you.
³ For I am the Lord your God,
The Holy One of Israel, your Savior;
I gave Egypt for your ransom,
Ethiopia and Seba in your place.
⁴ Since you were precious in My sight,
You have been honored,
And I have loved you;
Therefore I will give men for you,
And people for your life.
⁵ Fear not, for I am with you;
I will bring your descendants from the east,
And gather you from the west;
⁶ I will say to the north, 'Give them up!'

And to the south, 'Do not keep them back!'
Bring My sons from afar,
And My daughters from the ends of the earth—
[7] Everyone who is called by My name,
Whom I have created for My glory;
I have formed him, yes, I have made him."
[8] Bring out the blind people who have eyes,
And the deaf who have ears.
[9] Let all the nations be gathered together,
And let the people be assembled.
Who among them can declare this,
And show us former things?
Let them bring out their witnesses,
that they may be justified;
Or let them hear and say, "It is truth."
[10] "You are My witnesses," says the Lord,
"And My servant whom I have chosen,
That you may know and believe Me,
And understand that I am He.
Before Me there was no God formed,
Nor shall there be after Me.
[11] I, even I, am the Lord,
And besides Me there is no savior.
-Isaiah 43:1-11 (NKJV)

As I was reading this morning, I came to these passages. I had to stop and truly ponder them for several minutes, thinking of what God was actually saying here.

The beginning of this collection of verses makes our hearts realize that we do nothing which God does not already know or even intend. We go through situations and believe things just "happen." We suppose the cards just fall into place – from winning a contest to getting a clean bill of health; or a car accident to unbeknownst taxes.

We also tend to take responsibility for way too much. Our hard work helped us obtain a promotion and a raise. An excellent diet and exercise produced a healthy baby. The computer games and friends' influences eventually lured our teenagers to rebel. Don't get me wrong; we do have a part to play in the way things play out in our lives. I'm a big believer in owning what you do and your involvement in the outcome of events.

But God has the ultimate power. He is the final authority on what does and does not happen.

Take a look at what God is saying to Israel and to us in these verses. In verses three through eight, He states over and over again that He has declared everything – "former things from the beginning," "new things," and "hidden things." The God of Israel is the creator, the informer, the author of every single thing. And why? For His glory.

That was the part that really got me. Everything that happens to me, in my life, and in the world around me is for His glory.

His refining of me is for His sake. Which means when I am having a really hard time or when I go through a tragedy or disaster, it is for Him. In the past I have thought it was to make me a better person or maybe strengthen me for the next time. Thinking, "I will probably come out on the other side stronger and better." Those are side benefits. The purpose, however, is for Him, not me.

My entire life and every single thing happening is for Him to shine.

My wealth and prospering is to illuminate His splendor. The difficulties I work through are for His triumph to prevail. Sicknesses, deaths, and heartaches in my life are meant to bring complete and utter fame to His name. Not mine.

I find a bizarre peace in knowing that truth. Throughout

everything that happens in my life, I will become all He wants me to be – patient, content, stronger, better. But… He will get all the glory. That's the whole point!

WAIT: Acknowledge God's glory in every area of your life – good and bad.

CULTIVATE: Read Luke 1:10-14 and Revelation 21:23-24 and realize Jesus' life is enveloped in glory.

endurance.

※

³⁵ Therefore do not cast away your confidence, which has great reward. ³⁶ For you have need of endurance so that after you have done the will of God, you may receive the promise.
-Hebrews 10:35-36 (NKJ)

³⁵ Do not, therefore, fling away your fearless confidence, for it carries a great and glorious compensation of reward.

³⁶ For you have need of steadfast patience and endurance, so that you may perform and fully accomplish the will of God, and thus receive and carry away [and enjoy to the full] what is promised.
-Hebrews 10:35-36 (AMP)

※

Endurance. That's a loaded word. Look at the meaning of endurance in the dictionary.

> *1. the fact or power of enduring an unpleasant or difficult process or situation without giving way*

> *2. the ability or strength to continue or last, despite fatigue, stress, or other adverse conditions; stamina*
> *3. lasting quality; duration*

In the Amplified version of Hebrews, the word endurance is also prefaced with the words "steadfast patience".

We live in a culture that does not promote patience or endurance. Our days are filled with microwave ovens, cell phones, drive-thrus, and call waiting. When we get an illness, we want a speedy recovery. When our electricity suddenly shuts off, we expect the power company to fix it immediately. And heaven forbid our Internet goes down. We cannot function without instant access to our email or eBay or our daily (maybe hourly) dose of Facebook.

I'm not sure this is the way we were intended to operate – with instant gratification. God reiterates throughout scripture to be patient. Endure. Wait.

> Be still before the Lord and wait patiently for Him. -Psalm 37:7

> I wait for the LORD, my soul waits, and in his word I put my hope. -Psalm 130:5

> Endure hardship as discipline; God is treating you as sons. -Hebrews 12:7

Endure hardship with us like a good soldier of Christ Jesus. -2 Timothy 2:3

You too, be patient and stand firm. -James 5:8

Likewise, God's desire is not for us to seek an "easy out" when things are tough. It may be a hard decision about a different job or the stress of losing your current job. You may be going through a rough patch with your spouse or struggling to raise your kids. Whatever it is – a minor decision, an illness, a daily struggle, a dry season – the word for you today is endure.

Endure through the hardship. Be patient in the circumstance. Wait on the Lord, no matter how long and how much you want an answer. God is in the business of giving us exactly what we need when we need it. As you trust in Him, also trust in His word. Endurance is not an option, it's a command.

Trust in the plan that is already in motion. Endure.

WAIT: Wait on the Lord and endure patiently. Take a moment and breathe.

CULTIVATE: Write one of the short verses listed above on a note card. Place it in your car or on the fridge, so you can see it daily.

postcard.

⁳⁶ So Gideon said to God, "If You will save Israel by my hand as You have said— ³⁷ look, I shall put a fleece of wool on the threshing floor; if there is dew on the fleece only, and it is dry on all the ground, then I shall know that You will save Israel by my hand, as You have said." ³⁸ And it was so. When he rose early the next morning and squeezed the fleece together, he wrung the dew out of the fleece, a bowlful of water. ³⁹ Then Gideon said to God, "Do not be angry with me, but let me speak just once more: Let me test, I pray, just once more with the fleece; let it now be dry only on the fleece, but on all the ground let there be dew." ⁴⁰ And God did so that night. It was dry on the fleece only, but there was dew on all the ground.
-Judges 6:36-40 (NKJV)

I'm waiting for a postcard to arrive.

Over the past month my family has been dealing with a somewhat difficult decision. It's not a life or death matter, but more of a direction decision – which way is the Lord leading in the midst of a storm that is stirring around us.

My husband and I have been dealing with the issue privately for over a year, but we do know this is exactly where God wants us at the moment. He made it clear to us to stay in the middle of the storm. And so we did – until now.

Most people think they can endure tough times. (I'm not talking about a life-threatening illness or even some sort of catastrophe.) It sounds much easier than it is.

I'm speaking of the everyday dramas we face, the ones primarily that we create, not those forced upon us. Situations, such as changing jobs, purchasing a home, having a baby, or opening your home to a relative. I've been in all of the above places (some more than once). Even though we choose to put ourselves in the center of those circumstances, it is hard and can be stressful. This is the type of "tough time" I'm referencing.

I personally have sought God to give me direction, grant me some sort of release, or generate a change. Nothing... for a year.

Within that year, however, I have been at complete peace. I have had great rest. I have known extreme trust. Peace, rest, and trust in a God who has things under control. My relationship with Him has deepened during this time. In fact, I almost felt my "roots" extend into a safe, but secret place with the Lord Jesus. Then, as if the root knows when it's deep enough (for now), it stabilizes for the next change.

That next change is now upon us. The first thing that clued us in was our children. We have three teenage boys and a daughter not far behind. They started sensing God wanted to change some things in our life, and they voiced it to us. (That, in itself is a miracle, right?)

When our children feel like they are hearing from the Holy Spirit, we take notice – especially when it lines up with what we've been sensing for so long. Next, God directed us to seek counsel – people who knew of our situation, but did not have any benefit in the outcome. Last, we diligently sought the Word. Plain and simple.

Now, back to the postcard… We have the decision before us, and we are sure God is saying to make the transition. However, we are unsure of exactly the steps to take. So, I have asked the Lord for a fleece, a sign, something certain in my uncertainty – a postcard.

I told my family that I am expecting a postcard with something very specific for our situation within the next several weeks. It could be an advertisement, an invitation, or just a personal note. Nevertheless I anticipate it to be a clear word from Jesus.

So, I'm off to the mailbox.

WAIT: What are you waiting on from God? Ask Him.

CULTIVATE: Send someone a postcard today with a verse or word God tells you to extend. It may be the very sign they are waiting on.

ps - I received the postcard :)

light in dark.

"Blessed be the name of God,
   forever and ever.
He knows all, does all:
   He changes the seasons and guides history,
He raises up kings and also brings them down,
   he provides both intelligence and discernment,
He opens up the depths, tells secrets,
   sees in the dark—light spills out of him!
God of all my ancestors, all thanks! all praise!
   You made me wise and strong.
And now you've shown us what we asked for.
   You've solved the king's mystery."
-Daniel 2:20-23 (MSG)

The people who walked in darkness
   have seen a great light;
those who dwelt in a land of deep darkness,
   on them has light shone.
-Isaiah 9:2 (ESV)

For God, who said, "Let light shine out of darkness," has shone in our hearts to give the light of the knowledge of the

glory of God in the face of Jesus Christ.
-2 Corinthians 4:6 (ESV)

In the beginning there was darkness and God. Genesis 2:2 states that, "darkness was on the face of the deep. And the Spirit of God was…"

We tend to steer clear of the darkness. To most of us darkness means strange or scary or sad. However, there are just times when our lives emit little or no light. We sit in what seems like a dark, damp cell with no windows. We know the sun is shining; we just have not felt its warmth. There are birds singing, however we cannot hear the music. Flowers bloom and trees bud, but we are trapped in a season of darkness with no view and little hope.

However, God always starts His work in the dark.

Read that again. God always starts His work in the dark.

Always.

The earth was formed in the dark. The Exodus out of Egypt was in the middle of the night (Exodus 12:31). Jesus' birth was announced by night (Luke 2). The resurrection of our

Lord occurred while it was still dark (John 20:1).

You may be in a shadowy, black place right now. I have been there before, and I'm sure I will be there again. Whether the situation you are facing is a misfortune or a misdeed, God is there. Whether or not you can hear Him, see Him, or sense Him; God is there. Even if there seems no way out, no way through, and no way of salvation, God is there.

In the quiet, He is there.
In the blackness, He is there.
In the deep, dark places. He is there.

And He is working. He is pursuing your heart and your healing. He is making a way where there is no way. He is creating light out of your darkness. He is speaking into your silence. He is breaking through your bitterness. He is soothing your sadness.

God did not reveal light in the daytime. He used the darkness to display His glory and splendor. He started His greatest works throughout creation in what looked like bleak and barren conditions. Conditions similar to yours.

Rub the sleep out of your eyes. Someone is about to turn on the lights.

WAIT: Search the dark places of your heart and realize God is already there.

CULTIVATE: Go into a closet or pantry with no lights on and light one candle. Pray for Jesus to shine in and through your darkness.

cold season.

---

¹ O Lord, don't rebuke me in your anger or discipline me in your rage.

² Have compassion on me, Lord, for I am weak.

   Heal me, Lord, for my bones are in agony.

³ I am sick at heart.

   How long, O Lord, until you restore me?

⁴ Return, O Lord, and rescue me.

   Save me because of your unfailing love.

⁵ For the dead do not remember you.

   Who can praise you from the grave?

⁶ I am worn out from sobbing.

   All night I flood my bed with weeping,

   drenching it with my tears.

⁷ My vision is blurred by grief;

   my eyes are worn out because of all my enemies.

⁸ Go away, all you who do evil,

   for the Lord has heard my weeping.

⁹ The Lord has heard my plea; the Lord will answer my prayer.

¹⁰ May all my enemies be disgraced and terrified.

   May they suddenly turn back in shame.

-Psalm 6 (NLT)

Isn't funny how a cold works? I mean a really, bad cold – stuffed up sinuses, headache, fever. Everyone has one – a mild one, a severe one. Everyone has nursed someone else who's had one – a child, a spouse, a friend.

A cold must run its course. This common virus causes aches and pains and stays around way too long. No cure. Few treatments. More misery. You can treat the symptoms, but you cannot make it to away. And a cold is anything but "cold." Typically, you have a fever, so you're hot.

Spiritually speaking, it can hit you as well. The cold virus is a great illustration of the "cold" seasons that we will all go through at one time or another.

When you have a cold, your body's temperature does not correspond to the outside environment. There is a clash of balance. Everything can be going "right" in the world or with everyone else, yet you know things are not "right" with you. Something is **off**.

Also, as you nurse a cold, it's best to actually eat nutritious meals even though you rarely want to eat anything (except maybe chicken soup). In the same way, most of the time you don't feel like reading the Word or praying when you are in a "cold" season. However, reading and praying is exactly what is required for healing.

In addition, you need lots of water. It is essential to stay hydrated when you're sick. Living water, which is the Holy Spirit moving in your life is similar and is a ***must***. The water of the Spirit will quench the heat and reinvigorate your senses.

When you have a cold, all you feel like doing is curling up with blanket on the couch and zoning out. You don't feel like eating or even preparing something to eat. Maybe a couple of crackers and a little bit of juice, but that won't cut it. You need a hearty helping of chicken soup – filled with the meat of the scripture. You need a pitcher of water – sipping on the constant refreshment of the Holy Spirit.

During your "cold" season, don't neglect yourself. Don't tune out and turn off. Push through the aches and pains that life is doling out and allow God to nurse you back to health.

WAIT: Get your blanket and cuddle up with His Word today.

CULTIVATE: Send a get well card to someone you know who is in a cold season. Remind them God is in the business of healing and bringing us back to health.

budget.

◆

¹ Jesus told his disciples: "There was a rich man whose manager was accused of wasting his possessions. ² So he called him in and asked him, 'What is this I hear about you? Give an account of your management, because you cannot be manager any longer.'

³ "The manager said to himself, 'What shall I do now? My master is taking away my job. I'm not strong enough to dig, and I'm ashamed to beg— ⁴ I know what I'll do so that, when I lose my job here, people will welcome me into their houses.'

⁵ "So he called in each one of his master's debtors. He asked the first, 'How much do you owe my master?'

⁶ "'Nine hundred gallons of olive oil,' he replied.

"The manager told him, 'Take your bill, sit down quickly, and make it four hundred and fifty.'

⁷ "Then he asked the second, 'And how much do you owe?'

"'A thousand bushels of wheat,' he replied.

"He told him, 'Take your bill and make it eight hundred.'

8 "The master commended the dishonest manager because he had acted shrewdly. For the people of this world are more shrewd in dealing with their own kind than are the people of the light. 9 I tell you, use worldly wealth to gain friends for yourselves, so that when it is gone, you will be welcomed into eternal dwellings.

10 "Whoever can be trusted with very little can also be trusted with much, and whoever is dishonest with very little will also be dishonest with much. 11 So if you have not been trustworthy in handling worldly wealth, who will trust you with true riches? 12 And if you have not been trustworthy with someone else's property, who will give you property of your own?

13 "No one can serve two masters. Either you will hate the one and love the other, or you will be devoted to the one and despise the other. You cannot serve both God and money."

14 The Pharisees, who loved money, heard all this and were sneering at Jesus.
-Luke 16:1-14 (NIV)

I do not believe in budgets at all. I know they are good to have, and they help keep you disciplined. But, they are just so restricting. I feel like "the budget" is telling me what I can and cannot do, and I really don't want to live like that. I'm somewhat of a rebel (a big surprise to those who know me), and budgets just rub me the wrong way.

Most likely, what bothers me the most is if there's anyone messing up the budget, it's me. If we overspend, underpay, or go beyond our means it's usually my fault. And, once I screw up… well, the budget is shot, so it doesn't matter now, right?

Wrong! God continues to teach me this lesson over and over again. I just cannot seem to **get** it and stick to it. Do you know anyone who has a monthly budget, and she actually follows it with a fine-tooth comb? Her family will eat hot dogs for a month, if necessary. They will only order take-out pizza with a coupon or maybe not all. The air conditioning system stays turned off in the middle of the summer and the windows are open. Man, they are disciplined.

I am not that girl.

Nevertheless, God doesn't really care if I'm a rebel or if I don't like the way a budget "feels". He commands stewardship. All I have is from Him, and I need to be reminded of that truth – often. He wants me to be a good manager of the stuff – all of the stuff – He has generously given to me.

So, this month, I'm going to make a budget with my husband. I'm going to work really hard to stay within my means. (As far as my rebelliousness, I'm just going to have to get over it.) And, I'm going to try to honor God with my management of His stuff. I understand how fortunate I truly am, and it is my privilege to manage His stuff.

Thanks God, for the privilege!

WAIT: Focus on what God has allowed you to steward – a house, a car, or a paycheck.

CULTIVATE: Actually take an inventory of what the Lord has given you (on paper or in your head). Are you managing it well? In what areas could you improve?

light & momentary.

⁷ But we have this treasure in jars of clay to show that this all-surpassing power is from God and not from us. ⁸ We are hard pressed on every side, but not crushed; perplexed, but not in despair; ⁹ persecuted, but not abandoned; struck down, but not destroyed. ¹⁰ We always carry around in our body the death of Jesus, so that the life of Jesus may also be revealed in our body. ¹¹ For we who are alive are always being given over to death for Jesus' sake, so that his life may be revealed in our mortal body. ¹² So then, death is at work in us, but life is at work in you.

¹⁶ Therefore we do not lose heart. Though outwardly we are wasting away, yet inwardly we are being renewed day by day. ¹⁷ For our light and momentary troubles are achieving for us an eternal glory that far outweighs them all. ¹⁸ So we fix our eyes not on what is seen, but on what is unseen. For what is seen is temporary, but what is unseen is eternal.
-2 Corinthians 4:7-12, 16-18 (ESV)

These verses, especially verses 16 through 18, have always been my favorite. My first couple of years as a Christian were very difficult. I had totally walked from death to life and because of that, not many friends or family members were standing by me. They were happy for me, similar to being happy for someone when they get a good grade on a test. Their thinking… "It's great for her, but that doesn't affect me." So, the happiness is from a distance – it's not relatable.

During that time, I struggled – and for a newly graduated, 18-year-old, it was extremely difficult. I disconnected from most of my friends. My family thought it was a "phase", so they paid little attention to me. My daily habits radically changed.

I started counseling for a mound of childhood issues I had to come to terms with. Soon thereafter, my boyfriend broke up with me, and I quit college. I was going through an immense amount of emotional and physical pain. So, I turned to the Word. At some point in the midst of the agony, God showed up. It was one of the first times that He spoke to me through the Bible.

As I read these verses, I felt comfort. I sensed reassurance. I realized hope. The situations I was experiencing were "light and momentary." And they were full of purpose. My so-called troubles were actually part of God's plan; His greater plan which was designed to develop something beautiful and eternal. What a concept! My temporary problems were being used to cultivate faith, nurture growth, and strengthen my relationship with Jesus.

Meditate on that for a moment. Every problem purposed.

I came to understand something amazing in my early walk with the Lord (it wasn't really a walk then, I was totally crawling). I knew in order for me to view life's disgraces, disappointments, and disasters correctly, I had to center my attention on Jesus. I had to focus on what was unseen. This had to be done on a daily basis.

It is so easy to divert our attention to the tangible. If we feel it, it must be real. It must take precedence in our heart. We are prone to pay attention to anything that makes us feel – hurt, love, grief, happiness. However, God wants us to direct our heart toward something that doesn't involve feelings. Our feelings deceive us. We hurt and believe it's never going end. We love and believe it will last forever. We grieve and cannot see the light at the end of the tunnel. We base our existence on feelings.

God wants us to fix our attention and our heart on Him. He is the only thing that will last. All of our earthly trials and tests are so temporal and temporary. By placing the spotlight on Jesus instead of our problems, we realize how small our problems are.

They grow dim in the light of Him.

WAIT: Consider your light and momentary troubles, and carry each of them to Jesus.

CULTIVATE: Email, text, or send verses 16-18 to someone today. It is always a good reminder to fix our eyes on Him and not here.

excuses.

---

¹ Then Job spoke again:
² "My complaint today is still a bitter one,
   and I try hard not to groan aloud.
³ If only I knew where to find God,
   I would go to his court.
⁴ I would lay out my case
   and present my arguments.
⁵ Then I would listen to his reply
   and understand what he says to me.
⁶ Would he use his great power to argue with me?
   No, he would give me a fair hearing.
⁷ Honest people can reason with him,
   so I would be forever acquitted by my judge.
⁸ I go east, but he is not there.
   I go west, but I cannot find him.
⁹ I do not see him in the north, for he is hidden.
   I look to the south, but he is concealed.
¹⁰ "But he knows where I am going.
   And when he tests me, I will come out as pure as gold.
¹¹ For I have stayed on God's paths;
   I have followed his ways and not turned aside.
¹² I have not departed from his commands,

>   but have treasured his words more than daily food.
> ¹³ But once he has made his decision, who can change his mind?
>   Whatever he wants to do, he does.
> ¹⁴ So he will do to me whatever he has planned.
>   He controls my destiny.
> ¹⁵ No wonder I am so terrified in his presence.
>   When I think of it, terror grips me.
> ¹⁶ God has made me sick at heart;
>   the Almighty has terrified me.
> ¹⁷ Darkness is all around me;
>   thick, impenetrable darkness is everywhere.
>
> -Job 23 (NLT)

We are a people of justice, or at least of justifying. All right, maybe not justifying – maybe excuses. We are always trying to plead our case on some issue. We all do it; and probably much more often than we think.

I have some personal favorites. (By the way, these are *my* excuses. Not trying to get in *your* stuff... Okay, maybe I am. :)

- I'm not going to try to read that story to my kids because they're not going to listen anyway. They'd rather watch TV.

- It really doesn't matter if I eat unhealthy food and don't exercise. High cholesterol runs in my family; there's nothing I can do about it.
- We're not going to church today because we've heard that sermon before. I just need some down time.
- It's not a good idea to have sex tonight because I'm too tired and I can't fully enjoy it. He should understand that.
- I'm not going to pray for that person because I'm sure they are ever going to change anyway.

We have excuses for everything, and we use them constantly – even if it's only in our head.

God is not swayed, though. He does not care about our excuses, even if they are good ones. Even if they are valid (in our own minds). His concern is for our obedience, our faithfulness, and our righteousness (our right standing with Him).

Our excuses probably sound like fingernails on a chalkboard – just an annoying noise that accomplishes nothing. When we make excuses – whether it's to our kids, our spouse, God, or ourselves – it is like Job searching for God in verses eight and nine. It's like talking to the wind. At the end of the day, our excuses are empty.

Excuses are our doubts about something we're not courageous enough to attempt (parent, work, etc.). They are our defense when we feel vulnerable. They are our disguises when we do not want to reveal what's under the mask.

Ouch.

God wants us to learn from Job and not expect Him to "hear our case." He is God, and He controls our destiny. He asks for our all – no shortcuts, no justifications, no rationalizations. He expects obedience – whether it's in the area of our health, our family, or our finances.

No more excuses. Follow through.

WAIT: What areas do you need to follow through in? Take them to God.

CULTIVATE: Send a note of encouragement to someone who might be making excuses in their life. Spur them on to follow through!

all of You.

¹ What shall we say then? Are we to continue in sin that grace may abound? ² By no means! How can we who died to sin still live in it? ³ Do you not know that all of us who have been baptized into Christ Jesus were baptized into his death? ⁴ We were buried therefore with him by baptism into death, in order that, just as Christ was raised from the dead by the glory of the Father, we too might walk in newness of life.

⁵ For if we have been united with him in a death like his, we shall certainly be united with him in a resurrection like his. ⁶ We know that our old self was crucified with him in order that the body of sin might be brought to nothing, so that we would no longer be enslaved to sin. ⁷ For one who has died has been set free from sin. ⁸ Now if we have died with Christ, we believe that we will also live with him. ⁹ We know that Christ, being raised from the dead, will never die again; death no longer has dominion over him. ¹⁰ For the death he died he died to sin, once for all, but the life he lives he lives to God. ¹¹ So you also must consider yourselves dead to sin and alive to God in Christ Jesus.
-Romans 6:1-11 (ESV)

More of You. Less of me.

As I was praying in my car last week, this popular Christian saying came to mind. I have actually been asking God for more Him and a lot of less of me. There was a quiet moment when I wasn't overthinking or overpraying. I was actually listening. I sensed the Lord say...

All of Me. None of you.

That is quite different. Read it again. Slower.

All of Me. None of you.

Scripture tells us something we all know. In Psalm 14:3 it states, "There is none who does good, no, not one." Paul reiterates this in Romans 3:12, but we truly do not need Paul to tell us this. We struggle. We stall. We sin. We are very aware of our "ungoodness."

Precisely the point why God needs none of us. And why we need all of Him.

I can look at my own daily life and get frustrated with myself. My feelings get hurt when my husband works a little too late. My emotions run high when the kids are procrastinating with their homework. My attitude can be swayed if the weather is yucky, if the bonus check doesn't come through, or the dog throws up. This earthly vessel is full of "herself" the majority of the time.

So, I pray for more of Jesus and less of me. However, less of me still means there is "me" in the container. The Lord revealed to me that when there is anything in the vessel besides Him, it is not pure and holy. Therefore, whatever I pour out (in my words or actions) has a good chance of being contaminated.

We have one of those single cup coffee makers. Every few months it has to be cleaned out because residue builds up. The instructions recommend flushing the system with 48 ounces of vinegar then running about three to four containers of water to completely flush the system.

So, that's what I do. Yet, every time I finish the fourth container of water I can still smell the slightest scent of vinegar. The bitterness hits me like strong Easter egg dye, and there is no way I'm making a tasty cup of coffee. My senses tell me that even the most miniscule amount of vinegar will ruin any good cup of joe. One, two, sometimes three more cycles of water are required before this coffee maker is in business again.

I'm amazed that such a small amount of vinegar can wreck a warm cup of coffee. It can. And any small amount of "us" can prevent the perfection of Christ from being realized in our lives.

All of Him.
None of us.

All of You, Jesus.
None of me.

WAIT: Ask the Lord to flush your earthly vessel and clean out the "you" that gets in the way of Him.

CULTIVATE: Write down areas where you are still contaminating your daily life. Write Jesus over each area – bolder and bigger.

darkness singing.

~~~
[ornament]
~~~

¹¹ And do this, understanding the present time. The hour has come for you to wake up from your slumber, because our salvation is nearer now than when we first believed. ¹²The night is nearly over; the day is almost here. So let us put aside the deeds of darkness and put on the armor of light. ¹³ Let us behave decently, as in the daytime, not in orgies and drunkenness, not in sexual immorality and debauchery, not in dissension and jealousy. ¹⁴Rather, clothe yourselves with the Lord Jesus Christ, and do not think about how to gratify the desires of the sinful nature.
-Romans 13:11-14 (NIV)

⁷ Because the Sovereign LORD helps me,
    I will not be disgraced.
    Therefore have I set my face like flint,
    and I know I will not be put to shame.
⁸ He who vindicates me is near.
    Who then will bring charges against me?
    Let us face each other!
    Who is my accuser?
    Let him confront me!

⁹ It is the Sovereign LORD who helps me.
    Who is he that will condemn me?
    They will all wear out like a garment;
    the moths will eat them up.
¹⁰ Who among you fears the LORD
    and obeys the word of his servant?
    Let him who walks in the dark,
    who has no light,
    trust in the name of the LORD
    and rely on his God.
¹¹ But now, all you who light fires
    and provide yourselves with flaming torches,
    go, walk in the light of your fires
    and of the torches you have set ablaze.
    This is what you shall receive from my hand:
    You will lie down in torment.
-Isaiah 50:7-11 (NIV)

This morning, I was awake earlier than normal. I decided to read my Bible and finish the last chapter of a John Piper book I'd been reading. As I finished and set the books aside, I looked toward the window. Complete darkness. I was in our family room which faces the backyard so no streetlights were visible. The moon had long moved across the sky behind a blanket of clouds. Nothing illuminated the yard or even the windowsill. Darkness. But, not silence.

Several birds had gathered outside; in a tree or perched on the deck railing or possibly atop a birdhouse. They could not be seen, but their gladsome greetings could be heard bright and clear. Songs in the midst of stillness. Glimmers flashing through the gloom. Dawn breaking the dark of night.

The scriptures beckon us to wake up and grasp the realization that our salvation is nearer now than it was – last week, yesterday, or even an hour ago. Not the salvation of being saved when you gave your life to the Lord Jesus (Ephesians 2:8), but the growing in your journey with God or the "working out your salvation."

> Therefore, my dear ones, as you have always obeyed [my suggestions], so now, not only [with the enthusiasm you would show] in my presence but much more because I am absent, work out (cultivate, carry out to the goal, and fully complete) your own salvation with reverence and awe and trembling. –Philippians 2:12 (AMP)

This salvation could also mean the saving grace needed during a dark season in life. We've all had them... perhaps a depressive state that just doesn't seem to go away. God reveals His truth – whatever we're going through is nearly over. Maybe not in our timing and possibly not the way we would have planned. In the grand scheme of life, though, it is nearly over and "the day is almost here." That is good news!

As we look expectantly for the dawn, we are also to engage in active faith. In Isaiah 50:7, we are directed to "set our face as flint" and trust Him.

Completely. In the darkness.

I love verse 10 in the Amplified version. It states for he "who walks in darkness and deep trouble and has no shining splendor [in his heart]? Let him rely on, trust in, and be confident in the name of the Lord, and let him lean upon and be supported by his God."

This is in the middle of the misery; in the grip of grief; in the depth of despair. While we're in a pitch black period, we rely on God Almighty. We trust in His name. We lean on Him for support and know that the night is nearly over.

It may be cloudy where you are with few rays of sunshine. It may be gloomy with dark storms hovering overhead. Or it may be pitch black with no signs of hope.

Birds are singing. Listen.

WAIT: Truly listen to birds singing – outside and in your heart.

CULTIVATE: Sit in the darkness – in the middle of the night or in a dark room. Focus on hearing the sound of God's voice and breathing in His spirit. Let Him remind you dawn is coming.

baby steps.

¹ Moses objected, "They won't trust me. They won't listen to a word I say. They're going to say, 'God? Appear to him? Hardly!'"

² So God said, "What's that in your hand?"

"A staff."

³ "Throw it on the ground." He threw it. It became a snake; Moses jumped back—fast!

⁴⁻⁵ God said to Moses, "Reach out and grab it by the tail." He reached out and grabbed it—and he was holding his staff again. "That's so they will trust that God appeared to you, the God of their fathers, the God of Abraham, the God of Isaac, and the God of Jacob."

⁶ God then said, "Put your hand inside your shirt." He slipped his hand under his shirt, then took it out. His hand had turned leprous, like snow.

⁷ He said, "Put your hand back under your shirt." He did it, then took it back out—as healthy as before.

⁸⁻⁹ "So if they don't trust you and aren't convinced by the first sign, the second sign should do it. But if it doesn't, if even after these two signs they don't trust you and listen to your message, take some water out of the Nile and pour it out on the dry land; the Nile water that you pour out will turn to blood when it hits the ground."

¹⁰ Moses raised another objection to God: "Master, please, I don't talk well. I've never been good with words, neither before nor after you spoke to me. I stutter and stammer."

¹¹⁻¹² God said, "And who do you think made the human mouth? And who makes some mute, some deaf, some sighted, some blind? Isn't it I, God? So, get going. I'll be right there with you—with your mouth! I'll be right there to teach you what to say."

¹³ He said, "Oh, Master, please! Send somebody else!"

¹⁴⁻¹⁷ God got angry with Moses: "Don't you have a brother, Aaron the Levite? He's good with words, I know he is. He speaks very well. In fact, at this very moment he's on his way to meet you. When he sees you he's going to be glad. You'll speak to him and tell him what to say. I'll be right

there with you as you speak and with him as he speaks, teaching you step by step. He will speak to the people for you. He'll act as your mouth, but you'll decide what comes out of it. Now take this staff in your hand; you'll use it to do the signs."
-Exodus 4:1-17 (MSG)

Most of us do not move forward into something new because… well… because it's new. It may be an area we're unfamiliar with, unskilled at, or unenthusiastic about.

My first two sons were completely different in how they approached walking. Reece, the oldest, was extremely cautious as he learned to pull himself up. He held onto the sofa or the wall constantly. If he started falling, he would lean toward an object and gently ease himself down so not to drop too quickly. He had no desire to crash and burn. (His technique was entirely too composed for a one-year-old.) Throughout his life, he has moved toward most ventures in the same manner. Often, it has been more harm than help. Even today, he tends to hesitate and procrastinate.

My other son, David, started walking with no reluctance. He stepped off couches and stairs with no thought of how far he might fall. He never cried or conceded. If he toppled over, he'd get back up and try again. His journey in life has been similar. David takes risks and is not afraid to fall or fail. He gets back up and keeps going.

Our entire life is brimming with baby steps; not only in the physical, but in our spiritual development as well. God is completely okay with that. In fact, He expects it.

As our children learn to walk, swim, ride a bike, or drive a car, we do not demand for them to become experts immediately. We are well aware that learning something takes time. It takes practice. It's a process. We instinctively have patience, whether they are restrained or reckless in their learning. We anticipate the baby steps.

As adults, we assume we've evolved or matured beyond the baby years. However, God may place a new calling on our life or lead us in a different direction. It possibly (and probably) will require instruction, discipline, and patience – on **our** part. We may need to make small strides on the way to the destination.

Moses was not a speaker. He did not want to be the one to confront Pharaoh. And, he definitely did not aspire to be the leader of the Exodus. But God called him, and He **was** going to equip him. (Moses wasn't quite on board with the plan yet.) I love the last part of the passage in The Message version:

"I'll be right there with you as you speak and with him as he speaks, teaching you step by step."

Step by step.

Our Father is so gracious and patient. He completely understands that we are not always ready for the next mission or the next movement. It may be a new year's resolution or a God-sized revelation that you know you must move toward. It will require baby steps. One day at a time; one moment at a time. Don't underestimate the situation, but don't let it overwhelm you either.

God's there. Step by step.

WAIT: Is God awakening you to a new adventure? Be okay with taking baby steps. He's there.

CULTIVATE: Ponder and plan what steps you need to take next. Write down the plan, step-by-step if necessary, and be patient as God provides and prepares.

comfort zone.

"Don't look for shortcuts to God. The market is flooded with surefire, easygoing formulas for a successful life that can be practiced in your spare time. Don't fall for that stuff, even though crowds of people do. The way to life—to God!—is vigorous and requires total attention.
-Matthew 7:13-14 (MSG)

15-16 So let's keep focused on that goal, those of us who want everything God has for us. If any of you have something else in mind, something less than total commitment, God will clear your blurred vision—you'll see it yet! Now that we're on the right track, let's stay on it.
17-19 Stick with me, friends. Keep track of those you see running this same course, headed for this same goal. There are many out there taking other paths, choosing other goals, and trying to get you to go along with them. I've warned you of them many times; sadly, I'm having to do it again. All they want is easy street. They hate Christ's Cross. But easy street is a dead-end street. Those who live there make their bellies their gods; belches are their praise; all they can think of is their appetites.
-Philippians 3:15-19 (MSG)

I dare you to get out of your comfort zone. I dare you to do something out of the ordinary this week. I dare you to take a risk for the sake of Christ.

We sit in our homes, our offices, and our churches – day after day, week after week, year after year. We do everything in our power to stay comfortable. We buy recliners, Sleep Number® beds, and universal remote controls to increase our relaxation.

Our lives are filled with the predictable. Most days are like the day before. We enjoy living in the rut (whether we want to admit it or not). We are creatures of habit. We work to keep our routines on track.

God wants us out of the rut, off the beaten path, and outside the box. His desire is for us to break out of our comfort zone. Jesus' life was anything but ordinary and monotonous. His days were never the same.

He had moments of rest.
> Then Jesus said, "Let's go off by ourselves to a quiet place and rest awhile." He said this because there were so many people coming and going that Jesus

and his apostles didn't even have time to eat. So they left by boat for a quiet place, where they could be alone. -Mark 6:30-32 (NLT)

He spent entire days teaching and healing.
Jesus traveled throughout the region of Galilee, teaching in the synagogues and announcing the Good News about the Kingdom. And he healed every kind of disease and illness.
-Matthew 4:23 (NLT)

He also stepped "out the box" of his culture – healing on the Sabbath (Matthew 12:9-13), talking to a foreign woman (John 4:1-30), and welcoming children (Luke 18:15-17).

As Christians, we can sometimes fall into an everyday practice of placing our pleasure above God's purpose. We settle for the good of our well being without seeking Christ's wellspring of wisdom (Proverbs 18).

C.S. Lewis states it best in <u>The Weight of Glory</u>.
"We are half-hearted creatures, fooling about with drink and sex and ambition when infinite joy is offered us, like an ignorant child who wants to go on making mud pies in a slum because he cannot imagine what is meant by the offer of a holiday at the sea. We are far too easily pleased."

Don't sleep, settle, or shy away from the amazing adventure God wants to give to you. Take a deep breath and break out of the box – today!

WAIT: Think about areas where you can step out of your comfort zone. Where is God leading you?

CULTIVATE: Write 3-5 risks or "out-of-the-box" experiences on separate small sheets of paper and place them in a box (a jewelry box or small gift box). Consider choosing one a week for the next month.

sacrifice.

ⁱ⁸ That day Gad came to David and said to him, "Go up and build an altar to the Lord on the threshing floor of Araunah the Jebusite." ¹⁹ So David went up to do what the Lord had commanded him.

²⁰ When Araunah saw the king and his men coming toward him, he came and bowed before the king with his face to the ground. ²¹ "Why have you come, my lord the king?" Araunah asked. David replied, "I have come to buy your threshing floor and to build an altar to the Lord there, so that he will stop the plague."

²² "Take it, my lord the king, and use it as you wish," Araunah said to David. "Here are oxen for the burnt offering, and you can use the threshing boards and ox yokes for wood to build a fire on the altar. ²³ I will give it all to you, Your Majesty, and may the Lord your God accept your sacrifice."

²⁴ But the king replied to Araunah, "No, I insist on buying it, for I will not present burnt offerings to the Lord my God that have cost me nothing." So David paid him fifty pieces of silver for the threshing floor and the oxen.
-2 Samuel 24:18-24 (NLT)

⁹ And let us not grow weary of doing good, for in due season we will reap, if we do not give up. ¹⁰ So then, as we have opportunity, let us do good to everyone, and especially to those who are of the household of faith.
-Galatians 6:9-10 (ESV)

But if anyone does not provide for his relatives, and especially for members of his household, he has denied the faith and is worse than an unbeliever.
-1 Timothy 5:8 (ESV)

Sacrifice: *an act of giving up something valued for the sake of something else regarded as more important or worthy; give up (something important or valued) for the sake of other considerations.*

Sacrifice is a noun **and** a verb. It is a thing or a feeling as well as an act. The American church knows little in regards to sincere sacrifice.

Our parking lots are packed with SUVs and reserved spaces for church staff. We like our sanctuaries full of well-dressed people and free of crying babies. (We don't want any distractions from hearing the Lord.) We give offerings for the building fund and for Operation Christmas Child, but we always make sure we have enough to pay our rent and purchase our own presents. (Just being honest, folks.) Few of us, including myself, truly give everything. A handful of us give over and above to the point of sacrifice. (I'm usually not one of those people.)

There is more to sacrifice than giving money. We can give up time, our talents, or our things. What I'm talking about, though, is surrendering something of value in a ***big*** way.

When my four children were all under the age of eight, my grandmother came to visit during the Christmas holidays. She stayed with us for about two weeks, and throughout that time we realized her dementia had worsened, and she needed 24 hour care. Her condition was not severe enough for an assisted-living facility (nor did we have the money for that option), but she could no longer live on her own. Most family members had full-time jobs and other professional responsibilities. I was a stay-at-home mom with an extra bedroom in our house, so that made us the most logical choice.

Before we made this major decision to relocate her, we prayed about it and asked others for wise counsel. Everyone we talked to said, "No way. Don't do it." Each person had good intentions. With young kids and a husband who traveled periodically, they feared it might be overwhelming. My grandmother's health was only going to intensify which could possibly lead to a great deal of weight and anxiety for me. They were honestly concerned for my well-being.

We wrestled with the decision. She's family. Shouldn't we sacrifice? What would Jesus do? (We truly asked ourselves **that** question.)

There was one couple in our small group who were preparing to be lifelong missionaries. We asked them their thoughts.

They said, "You absolutely should do it!" Their reasoning was… she's family, it is a sacrifice, and it's exactly what Jesus would do.

We did it.

It was the hardest four years of my life. There were days full of frustration and tears and sometimes fighting. As her memory slowly faded, her body followed close behind. She fell often, ate little, and became detached (never quite sure who we were). I listened to her complaints every single day, nursed her after surgeries, and assisted her in showering and going to the restroom. Things I never thought I'd do.

The years that my cantankerous grandmother lived with us taught me genuine mercy, grace, and love. God **had** given me more than I could handle. His desire was for me to completely rely on Him for my every day existence. I did. He **did** want me to give up my time, my money, and my comforts to care for someone else. I did. His purpose was to grow me to be more like Christ, who already gave the ultimate sacrifice. I'm getting there.

God is not concerned with our having enough. He **is** enough. He knows we can only grow and mature and experience the richness of His grace when we give ourselves away. Completely. A true sacrifice.

WAIT: God probably is calling you to sacrifice more in some area. Consider ways to give more to Him – sacrificially.

CULTIVATE: The Lord desires for us to give toward our family and our family of faith first. If the opportunity arises, to do something extraordinary (that might require sacrifice). Really think through it, and then do it!

scars.

---

³³ And when they came to the place that is called The Skull, there they crucified him, and the criminals, one on his right and one on his left. ³⁴ And Jesus said, "Father, forgive them, for they know not what they do."
-Luke 23:33-34 (ESV)

¹⁴ Strive for peace with everyone, and for the holiness without which no one will see the Lord. ¹⁵ See to it that no one fails to obtain the grace of God; that no "root of bitterness" springs up and causes trouble, and by it many become defiled."
-Hebrews 12:14-15 (ESV)

²¹ Then Peter came to him and asked, "Lord, how often should I forgive someone who sins against me? Seven times?" ²² "No, not seven times," Jesus replied, "but seventy times seven!

²³ "Therefore, the Kingdom of Heaven can be compared to a king who decided to bring his accounts up to date with servants who had borrowed money from him. ²⁴ In the process, one of his debtors was brought in who owed

him millions of dollars. ²⁵ He couldn't pay, so his master ordered that he be sold—along with his wife, his children, and everything he owned—to pay the debt.

²⁶ "But the man fell down before his master and begged him, 'Please, be patient with me, and I will pay it all.' ²⁷ Then his master was filled with pity for him, and he released him and forgave his debt.

²⁸ "But when the man left the king, he went to a fellow servant who owed him a few thousand dollars. He grabbed him by the throat and demanded instant payment.

²⁹ "His fellow servant fell down before him and begged for a little more time. 'Be patient with me, and I will pay it,' he pleaded. ³⁰ But his creditor wouldn't wait. He had the man arrested and put in prison until the debt could be paid in full.

³¹ "When some of the other servants saw this, they were very upset. They went to the king and told him everything that had happened. ³² Then the king called in the man he had forgiven and said, 'You evil servant! I forgave you that tremendous debt because you pleaded with me. ³³ Shouldn't you have mercy on your fellow servant, just as I had mercy on you?' ³⁴ Then the angry king sent the man to prison to be tortured until he had paid his entire debt.

[35] "That's what my heavenly Father will do to you if you refuse to forgive your brothers and sisters from your heart."
-Matthew 18:21-35 (NLT)

※

Forgiveness is easier said than done. We know we **should** forgive, but it's SO hard.

Some of us have been wronged unjustly. Others have brought on reactions or revenge that led down a path of resentment.

Maybe you've been physically or emotionally hurt – more than likely both. Parents, siblings, spouses, children, and friends have wounded us. Our heart holds onto each insult and injury. We try to forget and move forward, but we can't. The memories of the heartache and heartbreak are usually too deep, too distressing, and too damaging. It's human nature to guard our heart, so when wrong is done we build walls and bury hope.

There are people in our lives, right now, who *need* forgiveness. No matter what they did. No matter the severity of the scars. No matter the intention or the justification. They may not have apologized or acknowledged the offense. Maybe they disregarded or denied the event entirely. Mercy is still necessary.

True forgiveness is absolution. *You* have the power to give absolute pardon and complete release to another person. No strings attached.

People all over the world forgive their perpetrators. The transgression may have involved neglect, violence, torture, murder, or slavery. We don't deny the cruelty of those claims. But, what about the everyday infractions *we* endure.

Disrespect. Lies. Harsh words. Judgment. Control. Rudeness. Pride. Assumptions. Betrayal. Division. Tempers. Silence.

We take offense when someone cuts us off on the freeway or when a person cuts off our conversation. We get our feelings hurt when we're ignored, insulted, or embarrassed. We hold onto grudges convincing ourselves we have grounds. We confuse the conduct of the violation as a characteristic of the wound. It is not.

I bear a sizeable scar from an invasive surgery. The tool used to create the incision is not relevant to the scar itself. It could have been a knife or a sharp pair of scissors. The instrument had no bearing on the infliction. What remained was a mark that signified a piece of my story.

I also bear a spiritual scar from years of molestation. The sadness and suffering I experienced as a young girl left an impression on my life. However, the guilty party had no ownership of the scar that I carried. What remained was a mark that signified a piece of my story.

God healed me physically after that surgical procedure, and He redeemed me spiritually from the injustice I sustained as a child.

My role was to trust Him. Allowing God to be the healer. Expecting God to take up my cause. Knowing God is judge ***and*** jury.

You may have blows or blemishes that you believe will never heal. Whatever tool was used to inflict the pain in your life, it has no bearing on your scars. The marks left behind will remain, however, they are a part of your story that God will redeem.

Bitterness has the potential to keep those scars raw and infectious. It will also hinder your healing. Forgiveness is more for *you* than for the person responsible. Mercy is the balm that releases a healing on the inside and out.

Forgive. The scar will signify a piece of your story, but freedom will bring you peace and then God gets the glory.

WAIT: Examine your heart and ask the Lord for the grace to forgive.

CULTIVATE: God may ask you to do something tangible to show your forgiveness (write a letter, make a phone call, or give a hug.) Listen to His prompting and follow through.

His image.

---

²⁶ Then God said, "Let us make man in our image, after our likeness. And let them have dominion over the fish of the sea and over the birds of the heavens and over the livestock and over all the earth and over every creeping thing that creeps on the earth."

²⁷ So God created man in his own image, in the image of God he created him; male and female he created them.

²⁸ And God blessed them. And God said to them, "Be fruitful and multiply and fill the earth and subdue it, and have dominion over the fish of the sea and over the birds of the heavens and over every living thing that moves on the earth." ²⁹ And God said, "Behold, I have given you every plant yielding seed that is on the face of all the earth, and every tree with seed in its fruit. You shall have them for food. ³⁰ And to every beast of the earth and to every bird of the heavens and to everything that creeps on the earth, everything that has the breath of life, I have given every green plant for food." And it was so. ³¹ And God saw everything that he had made, and behold, it was very good. And there was evening and there was morning, the sixth day.

-Genesis 1:26-31 (ESV)

In His image. What a concept! Each human being on the planet was created in the very image of the Godhead – the Father, the Son, and the Holy Spirit. When you review the first chapter of Genesis, you catch a glimpse of the characteristics that were innately placed in every person.

> We begin.
> We imagine.
> We dream.
> We consider.
> We observe.
> We design.
> We create.
> We name.
> We plant.
> We bless.
> We give.
> We commune.
> We finish.
> We rest.

And that's just at the start. Our astonishing attributes are imbedded within each one of us from the moment of conception; in fact, before conception (Psalm 139:16).

We are uniquely created beings. Our interaction with each other is full of contrast and conflict. We enhance, enrich, and inflame one another. It's what makes us beautiful.

Just think, some of us are better at imagining than at planting. Some can design while others are great at communication. We teach, sing, cook, drive, direct, administer, help, write, and a million other gifts we have been graced with. Our talents and giftings vary, but we each can do a lot of something and a little of something else. It's what we're made of. It's the very essence of who God is in every sense of the word.

Just take some time to watch a baby between the age of one and two years old. He spends his days literally trying to master every single action listed above. No one tells him he must create, but put a crayon in his hand and he will color on something – paper, a wall, your dining room table. Toddlers watch every action and interaction around them. They name their toys, play in the dirt, and try to talk before anything makes sense. Young children and their behavior magnify the true image in how we are made. They live with abandon, striving until they can master their talent.

We... (you!) were created in the image of the Almighty; with all of His incredible, irreplaceable, and incomparable traits. Open your eyes with the wonderment of a toddler and take in the blessing of that knowledge.

WAIT: What are your gifts or talents? How are you honoring God by using them?

CULTIVATE: Do something you're good at today. Paint, cook, write, or encourage. Something that God created you to do.

signs.

~~~~~~~~

⁵⁴ He also said to the crowds, "When you see a cloud rising in the west, you say at once, 'A shower is coming.' And so it happens. ⁵⁵ And when you see the south wind blowing, you say, 'There will be scorching heat,' and it happens. ⁵⁶ You hypocrites! You know how to interpret the appearance of earth and sky, but why do you not know how to interpret the present time?
-Luke 12:54-56 (ESV)

²⁸ "From the fig tree learn its lesson: as soon as its branch becomes tender and puts out its leaves, you know that summer is near. ²⁹ So also, when you see these things taking place, you know that he is near, at the very gates. ³⁰ Truly, I say to you, this generation will not pass away until all these things take place. 31 Heaven and earth will pass away, but my words will not pass away.

³² "But concerning that day or that hour, no one knows, not even the angels in heaven, nor the Son, but only the Father. ³³ Be on guard, keep awake. For you do not know when the time will come. ³⁴ It is like a man going on a journey, when he leaves home and puts his servants in charge, each with

his work, and commands the doorkeeper to stay awake. ³⁵ Therefore stay awake—for you do not know when the master of the house will come, in the evening, or at midnight, or when the rooster crows, or in the morning— ³⁶ lest he come suddenly and find you asleep. ³⁷ And what I say to you I say to all: Stay awake."
-Mark 13:28-37 (ESV)

The days of winter seem to give us some good sleeping weather. It's cold outside and warm in our bed. Clouds and rain and snow tend to make us want to curl up in front of a fire. The sun sets early and darkness shrouds the late part of each day.

Here are some interesting facts about sleeping:
- Sleep helps you remember important information.
- Lack of sleep can lead to psychological distress, depression, and anger.
- Some studies suggest women need up to an hour's extra sleep a night compared to men.
- While you sleep, tissue growth and repair occurs and energy is restored.
- During sleep you can strengthen memories, or "practice" skills learned while you were awake (it's a process called consolidation).

Sleeping is good for you, no doubt. I believe God designed it so we would have time to not only rest physically but also recharge emotionally and spiritually. During our winter seasons we are probably in need of renewal, regeneration, and remission – an actual break from the tides of life.

God wants you to rest. He desires to restore and establish your heart.

- Restore to me the joy of your salvation and grant me a willing spirit, to sustain me. -Psalm 51:12
- Yes, my soul, find rest in God; my hope comes from him. -Psalm 62:5
- Restore us, O God; let your face shine, that we may be saved! -Psalm 80:3
- My hand shall be established with him; my arm also shall strengthen him. -Psalm 89:21
- May the favor of the Lord our God rest on us; establish the work of our hands for us— yes, establish the work of our hands. -Psalm 90:17

The phase of pause – that is sometimes what I see winter as… a pause. An interim. A waiting. Rest and wait.

However, don't miss the signs. We get so comfortable in the bed, beneath the covers, and by the fire, we fail to see hints of spring. Tiny buds bursting through the ground or the grass hinting a new hue of green. Evidence of a new season emerging.

As you sit in this phase, do not neglect to look for signals of spring. You will feel the air shift and sense a spiritual stirring. It may be a slight sensation, but you will discern it… if you are awake.

Make sure not to sleep too long or too deep. The coldness, the darkness, and the emptiness can sometimes lead to numbness. Literally. Just like frostbite. It may sneak up on you, and you lose all awareness. Stay awake. Stay alert.

God is the God of all things new. New life. New mercies. New seasons.

WAIT: Make an effort to awaken your spirit to the signs around you.

CULTIVATE: Take a walk and look for the physical signs of change, and examine your heart before the Lord.

obedience.

---

[17] For the desires of the flesh are opposed to the [Holy] Spirit, and the [desires of the] Spirit are opposed to the flesh (godless human nature); for these are antagonistic to each other [continually withstanding and in conflict with each other], so that you are not free but are prevented from doing what you desire to do.

[18] But if you are guided (led) by the [Holy] Spirit, you are not subject to the Law.

[19] Now the doings (practices) of the flesh are clear (obvious): they are immorality, impurity, indecency,

[20] Idolatry, sorcery, enmity, strife, jealousy, anger (ill temper), selfishness, divisions (dissensions), party spirit (factions, sects with peculiar opinions, heresies),

[21] Envy, drunkenness, carousing, and the like. I warn you beforehand, just as I did previously, that those who do such things shall not inherit the kingdom of God.

[22] But the fruit of the [Holy] Spirit [the work which His presence within accomplishes] is love, joy (gladness), peace, patience (an even temper, forbearance), kindness, goodness (benevolence), faithfulness,

[23] Gentleness (meekness, humility), self-control (self-restraint, continence). Against such things there is no law
-Galatians 5:17-22 (AMP)

It is a new year. A new year brings reflection and resolution. For the past couple of years, I have not looked forward to the new year. It only reminded me of what I didn't accomplish; the projects I didn't complete; the areas where I was ignoring the Lord.

Don't get me wrong, I was attending church, having a quiet time, and worshipping Jesus... while I was in complete disobedience.

My transgression was not huge a violation like adultery. I was not instigating a major rebellion or division in my household. There were not fits of anger or drunkenness or jealousies. It was just simple disobedience to small requests that God had asked of me.

I was not following through... on purpose.

In Galatians 5:19-21, adultery is listed with hatred. Witchcraft is listed alongside selfishness. Orgies are listed right above strife. There are no levels of disobedience. Disobedience is disobedience.

We categorize in order to justify ourselves. It makes us feel better. And it lets us "off the hook" – or, so we think.

James 2:10 says, "For whoever shall keep the whole law, and yet stumble in one point, he is guilty of all." That means we have to keep it all. There is no sin higher or worse than any other. The Bible states that "obedience is better than sacrifice" in 1 Samuel 15:22. Obedience.

The definition of obedience: *agreeing to do what was asked; submitting to authority; complying with a rule or request with respect and reverence.*

Obedience.

It was something I had avoided. I thought if I didn't look that direction, I wasn't held responsible. Didn't God know that I was tired and having a rough year? Surely He understood that I didn't "have the faith." Of course, He noticed that my emotions and hormones were out of control. I was trying, but it was hard. He **got** that, right?

Obedience. That is what He required.

Jesus said in John 14:23-24, ""All who love me will do what

I say. My Father will love them, and we will come and make our home with each of them. Anyone who doesn't love me will not obey me."

But... I loved Jesus.

It has taken me over two years to confront this truth. I don't have to "feel" like obeying him. We require our children to obey us even when they don't "feel" like it. How are we any different? Why should I get any special treatment? Why am I exempt from obeying?

This new year brings new resolve. A firmness to seek the fruit of the Spirit. The purpose to pursue what God has asked of me. A courage and resolution to obey.

WAIT: Be honest with the Lord (and yourself) in areas you are refusing to obey.

CULTIVATE: Write down one area of your life Jesus is waiting on obedience. Ask Him for a verse or a word of encouragement; write those on the same paper and review it daily.

night season.

¹ Preserve me, O God, for in You I put my trust.

² O my soul, you have said to the LORD,
    "You are my Lord,
    My goodness is nothing apart from You."
³ As for the saints who are on the earth,
    "They are the excellent ones, in whom is all my delight."

⁴ Their sorrows shall be multiplied
    who hasten after another god;
    Their drink offerings of blood I will not offer,
    Nor take up their names on my lips.

⁵ O LORD, You are the portion of my inheritance and my cup;
    You maintain my lot.
⁶ The lines have fallen to me in pleasant places;
    Yes, I have a good inheritance.

⁷ I will bless the LORD who has given me counsel;
    My heart also instructs me in the night seasons.

⁸ I have set the LORD always before me;
  Because He is at my right hand I shall not be moved.
⁹ Therefore my heart is glad, and my glory rejoices;
  My flesh also will rest in hope.
¹⁰ For You will not leave my soul in Sheol,
  Nor will You allow Your Holy One to see corruption.
¹¹ You will show me the path of life;
  In Your presence is fullness of joy;
  At Your right hand are pleasures forevermore.
-Psalm 16 (NKJV)

As I was reading through my scheduled reading last week, my cross-references led me to Psalm 16. My week had already begun with a huge move of God in my heart. Our church began a five-week journey, which would include praying, fasting, and desperately seeking the Lord — not only for the future of our church, but also the city and our individual place within the bigger passion of our church's purpose.

While I was being obedient and reading and praying with regards to the church, God opened up truths to *me*. About me. For me. I wasn't ready for that; or so I thought.

My first daily Bible reading was Psalm 73. It's an awesome slice of scripture that reminds us that no matter what earthly "thing" is vying for our attention and adoration, God is all we need in heaven and on earth. Good stuff. Actually, great stuff! Take some time later to read Psalm 73.

In verse 26 of Psalm 73, my cross-reference listed Psalm 16:5, so I decided to read Psalm 16 in its entirety.

When I saw several places within the passage that were already underlined, I knew these words had spoken to me before in some fashion; maybe I had just forgotten. God was going to speak – maybe a reminder or something new. Either way I was excited.

My soul started stirring at the words in verse 5 (emphasis mine).

> ⁵ O LORD, You are the portion of my inheritance
>   and my cup; You maintain my lot.
> ⁶ The lines have fallen to me in pleasant places;
>   Yes, I have a good inheritance.
> ⁷ I will bless the LORD who has given me counsel;
>   My heart also instructs me in the ***night seasons***.

Night seasons… that resonated deep within me at that very moment. I finally had a name for where I had been over the past year. I have been living in a night season.

Here's what I think a "night season" means. This time is not necessarily a dark and depressing time. (I've had those.) It is not a season of loneliness like in a desert. (I've been in those, as well.) Flash back in your mind to a time when you were up in the middle of the night. It could have been to take care of a sick baby, to get away from a snoring husband, or just because your mind was racing with a to-do list that refused to let you rest. For the first 5-10 minutes, it's hard to see. You possibly run into a dresser or fumble with a doorknob. But after a short while, your eyes (and awareness) adjust in the dark. It becomes comfortable. It's amazing how much you are able to exist in a world with no light, no sound, and no clarity. It's so nice and quiet. You become adjusted to the shadows, the solitude, and the silence. So adjusted, that you may stay there… for quite a while.

That is a night season.

Night seasons tend to last a long time. Again, remember how it is when you awake in the middle of the night. If you are one of those who cannot go back to sleep easily, the night drags on. The sunrise is elusive. The clock slows to a snail's pace. Night seasons in our lives are similar. They creep and crawl seeming to take their own sweet time. We soon are in a place where we don't even notice anymore. We walk around in the dark, but since our senses have adjusted and we're somewhat satisfied, we reside… in the night season.

I believe it takes the Lord and His word to awaken us from that night season. He reminds us that He is our portion and our cup. He supports our lot (which means He guards all we are). Our hearts testify to His goodness, even in our night seasons.

For some of you, it's time to wake up. It's hard; like awakening from a really great dream you want to stay in. But God is not fulfilling all you are becoming in your dreams. He is the God of the living and the awake (Matthew 22:32).

Wake up! Dawn is coming. The sun is rising. The night season has run its course.

Good morning!

WAIT: Read Psalm 73.

CULTIVATE: Get up early and sit in the quietness with Jesus. Watch the sunrise, and realize the night season will come to an end.

come away.

⁸ The voice of my beloved!
  Behold, he comes,
leaping over the mountains,
  bounding over the hills.
⁹ My beloved is like a gazelle
  or a young stag.
Behold, there he stands
  behind our wall,
gazing through the windows,
  looking through the lattice.
¹⁰ My beloved speaks and says to me:
"Arise, my love, my beautiful one,
  and come away,
¹¹ for behold, the winter is past;
  the rain is over and gone.
¹² The flowers appear on the earth,
  the time of singing has come,
and the voice of the turtledove
  is heard in our land.
¹³ The fig tree ripens its figs,
  and the vines are in blossom;
  they give forth fragrance.
Arise, my love, my beautiful one,
  and come away.

-Song of Solomon 2:8-13 (ESV)

Seasons do not last. They come and make themselves known by particular weather patterns, varying temperatures, and specific events. Each period of time then sets the stage for the next step, the next chapter, the next season.

Some of us like the cold weather. We like to stay indoors and isolate. We wrap up in blankets and heavy clothing. We settle in and get comfy as the sky is forlorn and the ground is frozen.

In winter, we stay put.

In spite of this, God is calling you out of winter. He is looking at you through the window (verse nine) and motioning for you to join Him.

"Come away."

The Lord spoke this to me in the middle of actual winter - February 12th to be exact. I have it written in my Bible. For a couple of years I felt like I was in the wilderness. I was dry and parched. There was nothing that could quench my thirst. After a long time spent in the desert, my soul had become cold - almost numb. Winter started to set in, and I became comfortable and callous. My eyes and my heart stopped anticipating the seasonal shift. I had stopped sensing and become stagnant - almost frozen. Almost.

"Come away."

The Lord gently whispered through the frosty window. He was beckoning me to get up and go with Him. He told me that this season was passing and flowers were starting to appear. A new season, a new chapter, a new breakthrough was emerging. He was gesturing for me to come see it, just like a dad would do with his daughter or a bridegroom with his bride.

"Come."

Jesus is calling you. The snow is melting and small buds are blossoming. You cannot see them unless you go outside. You cannot smell the scent of spring unless you venture past the walls that have enclosed you. You cannot feel the crisp, clean hint of the Holy Spirit unless you heed His voice.

Get up. Throw off the blanket. Walk to the door. Listen.

"Come."

Go.

WAIT: Listen for the sweet voice of Jesus calling you. He is calling.

CULTIVATE: Go outside no matter the actual season, and spend time listening to the Lord.

your reflections.

"It is on December nights,
with the thermometer at zero,
that we most think of the sun."
Les Misérables

"If we had no winter,
the spring would not be so pleasant:
if we did not sometimes taste of adversity,
prosperity would not be so welcome."
Anne Bradstreet, British poet 1612-1672

verse index.

2 Corinthians 4:6	light in dark
2 Corinthians 4:7-12, 16-18	light & momentary
1 Samuel 17:36-51	giants
2 Samuel 24:18-24	sacrifice
1 Timothy 5:8	sacrifice
2 Timothy 2: 3	endurance
Colossians 2:6-10	dormant
Daniel 2:20-23	light in dark
Exodus 4:1-17	baby steps
Galatians 5:17-22	obedience
Galatians 6:9-10	sacrifice
Genesis 1:26-31	His image
Hebrews 10:35-36	endurance
Hebrews 12:7	endurance
Hebrews 12:14-15	scars
Isaiah 9:2	light in dark
Isaiah 41:17-20	the valley
Isaiah 43:1-11	His glory
Isaiah 50:7-11	darkness singing
Jeremiah 30:17-21	windows
Job 23	excuses
Judges 6:36-40	postcard

Luke 1:41-42	a girl
Luke 1:46-49	a girl
Luke 2:25-38	christmas
Luke 12:54-56	signs
Luke 16:1-14	budget
Luke 23:33-34	scars
Malachi 3:1-4	laundry
Mark 6:30-32	comfort zone
Mark 13:28-37	signs
Matthew 4:23	comfort zone
Matthew 6:25-33	wish list
Matthew 7:13-14	comfort zone
Matthew 18:21-35	scars
Matthew 24:32	dormant
Philippians 2:12	darkness singing
Philippians 3:15-19	comfort zone
Philippians 4:18-20	wish list
Psalm 6	cold season
Psalm 16	good night & night season
Psalm 18:1-19	storms
Psalm 23	the valley

Psalm 33:13-22	quilt
Psalm 37:7	endurance
Psalm 119:25-32	reflection
Psalm 130:5	endurance
Psalm 139:13-16	quilt
Romans 6:1-11	all of You
Romans 13:11-14	darkness singing
Song of Solomon 2:8-13	come away

about the author.

Janelle is a helpmeet to Michael and mom to four incredible blessings — Reece, David, Bryson and Nicolle. She is a genuine Southern girl from Chattanooga, TN. She and her husband founded in His image productions almost 18 years ago. Their family resides in the greater Atlanta area with their two yorkies, Sophie and Rocko.

Janelle and her family serve at Passion City Church and Passion Conferences on a regular basis. She is also the Jail Outreach Leader for Out of Darkness, a non-profit organization committed to the rescue and restoration of victims of commercial sexual exploitation.

Janelle enjoys running, reading, and traveling with her man. She truly understands the many seasons women journey through. She'd love to hear from you about your seasons. To learn more and connect with Janelle go to **www.graceunwrapped.com**.

GRACEunwrapped.com

janelle@graceunwrapped.com
speaker * author * cheergiver

Made in the USA
Charleston, SC
28 January 2014